All Things Homescho
180 Devotions for Homeschool

by Jan L. Burt

Rebecca—
Lord bless you!
Jan L. Burt

ISBN: 9781511556316

Godly Encouragement for Homeschooling Mothers
5021 Pembrook Court
Wichita, KS 67220
WWW.AllThingsHomeschool.weebly.com
WWW.MomsWhoHomeschool.blogspot.com

Cover image designed at Canva.com by Jan L. Burt

Week One, Day 1

<u>Romans 8:28</u> - And we know that in all things God works for the good of those who love him, who have been called according to his purpose.

This tried and true verse is oft quoted as a balm for those in a difficult season of life. It also contains a beautiful promise for homeschooling moms trudging along through circumstances that, while at times difficult, are not normally much more than simply full. Full of laundry and science experiments and trips to the library and runny noses. Full of hugs and read-alouds and laughter and joy. Full of all things homeschool; indeed, very full.

Do all things truly work for the good of those who love the Lord and are called by Him in the daily routine of a homeschool family? Of course the answer is "Yes", but how often do you think about the truth that every single part of your day is being worked out for your good by your loving God? Knowing the answer to a question is very different than believing that answer applies to you, right now, today.

Today, be sure to remember that the goodness of the Lord is for you and your children. He has worked, is working, and will continue to work all things for you. Why? Because you love Him and are called according to His purpose. And a big part of His purpose for you is homeschooling. Good has come, good is here today, and even more good is coming from Him for you in the future.

Be at peace in that knowledge today.

Psalm 19:7b - The statutes of the Lord are trustworthy, making wise the simple.

Many times over the course of nearly two decades of homeschooling, I have felt completely inept. Sometimes at teaching algebra, sometimes as to how I should parent a particular child at a particularly difficult time, sometimes as a wife and a friend.

It is during these times that I must listen, loud and clear, to what God's Word says. And I must block out what the world and my flesh say. How wonderful that Psalm 19:7 provides the promise that the Lord, who makes wise the simple, will enable me to complete the tough task of homeschooling! He will enable me to parent my children for His glory. My marriage will be blessed and He leads and guides me. Any friendships He is the center of will be as he desires they ought to be.

Submit and obey the Lord, believe that His statutes are trustworthy, and be blessed as you stay close to Him.

Week One, Day 3

I clearly recall the day God told me that homeschooling is my career assignment, delivered straight from Him, and it was high time I started acting like it.

I was sitting at piano lessons, listening to my daughter play, working on a to-do list for some upcoming summer events. As I pondered all I needed to get done in the near future, I realized the Lord was speaking to my heart about our family's homeschool. Laying aside the to-do list, I paused to listen to the Holy Spirit's gentle voice. His word to me was a reminder (mind you, it was a gentle yet *firm* reminder) that He had called me to homeschool. It was my job assignment, my commission, directly from God to me. I needed to act like it was my "career assignment" and take it seriously every day, working at it with all my heart and not leaving bits and pieces undone or pushed aside due to the more urgent demands from other areas of my life. In a nutshell, He told me to *act* the way I *said* I felt about homeschooling.

That was convicting, encouraging and refreshing all at the same time. If you have not heard from the Lord about your homeschool in a while, why not spend a few minutes praying right now? Ask Him to speak to you, and listen for His answer.

Let Him convict, encourage and refresh you today.

"Let us, then, take all our perplexities to Him and say, 'Lord, what wilt thou have me to do?' Leave not thy chamber this morning without enquiring of the Lord." – C. H. Spurgeon

I agree so strongly with this quote from Charles Haddon Spurgeon that I vehemently ask, "Why would a mother ever begin her day without first inquiring of the Lord for His will, His grace, and His strength?"

There will always be sleepless nights, early mornings, busy schedules, and the like to tempt us from seeking the Lord's presence at the start of each new day. But we have the choice to be with the Lord, even on days when we are praying while rocking a sick toddler or coping with sudden emergencies. Life does not cause us to neglect time with the Lord; we allow ourselves to be pulled away. Simply do not allow it, and you will find that it isn't so difficult to get away with the Lord after all.

We need Him every single day, don't we? And so we need to begin every single day asking Him what He would have us to do.

Seek Him today, be renewed in His presence, and commit to inquire of Him before you begin to rush about doing your daily work.

Week One, Day 5

    <u>James 4:2c</u> – You do not have, because you do not ask God.

    James 4:2 tells us that we have not because we ask not. There may be something you are missing, something you are lacking, simply because you have yet to ask the Father for it. You may not even know what that missing something is.

    Have you considered this verse before in direct relation to your homeschool? Your marriage? Your children? Your finances? Your health? God's Word applies to every aspect of our lives; there is no part over which He does not desire to reign.

    Spend some time in prayer, asking Him to reveal any situation where you have a lack. Then commit yourself to believing the promise of James 4:2.

    Ask Him for whatever it is that you need. Thank Him for His promise to hear you and to provide for you.

    Just ask. And be prepared to see Him answer.

Always be willing to submit your homeschool, and your children, to the Lord.

Anything that we cling to too tightly has the potential to become an idol. Actually, anything we are clinging to probably <u>is</u> an idol in our lives. And that means it is time to let it go.

But our hands become cemented and rigid and we cannot seem to open them enough to release that upon which we've taken hold. So we must ask the Lord to remove the idol from our grasp.

What if we don't want to let go? What if we don't feel as if we even want to ask Him to take it? Well then we ask Him to make us want to want to let go. He can give us the desire to lay aside our tightly-held idols. He will do it if we ask Him to.

Begin by asking Him what idols you are grasping (you may not even be aware until He reveals it to you). Then move forward with the Lord by allowing Him to loosen your grip in His own gentle way. Pray this through, for as long as it takes, in order to have your stiff hands laid open before the Lord. Then you will be able to receive what He has for you

Week Two, Day 2

"In one thousand trials it is not five hundred of them that work for the believer's good, but nine hundred and ninety-nine of them, AND ONE BESIDE." – George Mueller

Every single trial will work for the believer.

Not *against* the believer. *For* the believer.

Too often we sabotage this truth from Romans 8:28. We focus so much, with such intensity, on the trial that we are completely blind to God as He works to make that trial work for us.

God will not raise His voice to scream above the roaring din that is your thoughts. His Word speaks loudly enough, would we simply listen to it.

What does the Word of God say about the particular situation you are facing? Do not listen to the world, to the enemy, or even to anyone who contradicts the Bible. In every trial, in all of it, God will make the trial work for you. Listen only to Him.

Week Two, Day 3

<u>1 Peter 4:7b</u> – Therefore be of sober mind so that you may pray.

I doubt many believers would argue that prayer is a vital element in the Christian's life. But not as many would claim to always go about their prayer time with a "sober mind".

Too often we take our list of wants, needs, complaints to the Lord in prayer and do so without a soberness of mind. We simply make our requests without much thought to the condition of our hearts.

It is of the utmost importance to remember – to daily remember! – that while our God is a loving Father, He is also completely holy and righteous. If we forget these aspects of His nature, we fail to come before Him with the reverence and awe He is due.

Being of sober mind, or having self-control as I pray, keeps me focused on who God is rather than on what I want or even what I need. Because one enormously important and life-changing thing I have learned about prayer is this: in seeking God for the answers, I learn that He is what I seek…He is the one and only answer to every question, want, or need, after all.

Week Two, Day 4

Romans 13:14 – Rather, clothe yourselves with the Lord Jesus Christ, and do not think about how to gratify the desires of the flesh.

Our flesh is a greedy thing, never satisfied, never fully quieted. Always demanding, clamoring for MORE. When we gratify our flesh, it does nothing but add fuel to its fire.

Jesus came to deliver us from such a life of self-absorption and sin. Of course, we will not have total deliverance and peace in this life, because we live in a fallen world. But we can have deliverance on a smaller scale, and peace that passes all understanding.

His heart for us is to take His yoke upon us and have His peace daily. He wants freedom for us rather than captivity. And if He wants that for us, doesn't it stand to reason that we can seek Him for it, knowing He will give it?

Clothe yourself with Jesus; think about Him, pray His Word, never let Him be far from your thoughts. Invite Him into your discussions and your daily work. Listen to Him and obey what He tells you. *Clothe* yourself –cover yourself – blanket yourself in Jesus. By doing so you will not leave much room to gratify the flesh.

Week Two, Day 5

<u>Hosea 6:3a</u> – Let us acknowledge the Lord; let us press on to acknowledge him.

What an amazing verse! Here we are encouraged to acknowledge the Lord. And then we are told to "press on" to acknowledge Him!

We all know that we should start our day with the Lord. But do we press on to acknowledge Him throughout the day?

During the stressful math lesson, press on to acknowledge Him! While preparing lunch for your hungry brood, press on to acknowledge Him. When your little one gives you a sloppy kiss on the cheek, press on to acknowledge Him. And at the end of a tiring day, as you lean your head against your husband's shoulder, press on to acknowledge Him.

He is always right there with you, in the mundane and the exciting, in the joys and the sorrows. You will be so very blessed as you choose to continually press on and acknowledge Him.

Week Three, Day 1

Ecclesiastes 12:1a – Remember your creator in the days of your youth.

Homeschooling, for many Christians, is a means to raise our children up in the fear and admonition of the Lord. It allows time for in-depth study of the Bible, family devotions, and a Christian worldview applied to all studies and subjects.

I have found that this verse is perfect to pray for my children. Truly, what more could we ask than that they know and love the Lord and live their lives for Him? Well, actually, the "more" we can ask for is that they recognize Him as Lord an honor Him while they are still young.

It isn't necessary to have a dramatic testimony; living for Christ from a young age is truly the greatest testimony one can have!

And there is no need to sow wild oats. Our children will not miss out on anything by fleeing form sin all the days of their younger years!

So pray Ecclesiastes 12:1, and ask God to help your children remember their Creator before they acquire a "testimony".

Week Three, Day 2

Matthew 13:12a - Whoever has will be given more, and he will have an abundance.

What do you have that the Lord has already given you which you may not be using fully? Before you will be given more, you need to be sure you are using what you already have.

Don't think you have much to offer, as a mom who homeschools her children? Here are two things I guarantee you already have: time and love. Are you using your time wisely on a daily basis? In your daily homeschooling? Are you giving your love liberally? To your family and to others in your life?

Do these things, and use whatever else you may have in abundance for God's glory, and He will give you more – an abundance in return for your abundant giving.

He never fails to keep His promises, you can count on that!

Friendship.

What does that word mean to you? What immediately comes to mind?

Many homeschool families seek out like-minded friends for their children. But are we, as mothers, seeking out the very best types of friendships ourselves?

Common interests often govern friendships, and if interests change over time, the friendship may begin to fade away.

Other times, a mistake (particularly a mistake made publicly, for the whole world to see) will push a friendship to its demise. Have you ever experienced this personally? Oh how difficult and painful it can be.

Be wise in choosing friends; do not simply assume everyone has your best interests in mind. Yet also do not assume evil of everyone!

And of special importance, be the friend that Jesus has been to you. Don't abandon your "friends" if a public mistake makes you look silly by remaining in the friendship. Now, I must say that blatant rebellion and sin are not to be ignored or tolerated; true friends work at restoration and want holy living for their peers. Be cautious, don't excuse sin, but be a true friend all the same.

Being in healthy relationships with other people takes work, it takes grace and forgiveness, and it takes the mind of Christ. Be wise as a friend in the ways He is wise. And always put on love.

Week Three, Day 4

"Quiet waiting before God could save from many a mistake and from many a sorrow." – J. Hudson Taylor

Do you have an important decision to make? Or perhaps you have grown impatient with some aspect of life and are ready to bring about some type of change. Let me encourage you not to take any hasty action. Be certain the Lord is leading you before you move. If He isn't, then be still.

J.Hudson Taylor is very much correct in his estimation that many sorrow and mistakes could be avoided with quiet waiting before God. If you have not stilled yourself before Him, then how can you know what His will is? If you have not asked Him for His loving council and abundant wisdom, then you certainly will not have it. As James 4:2 says, you have not because you ask not.

Hold off on needless sorrow, stay pointless mistakes. Wait quietly before your God who loves you and know that He will direct your steps.

Week Three, Day 5

Proverbs 15:13 – A happy heart makes the face cheerful, but heartache crushes the spirit.

One piece of timely advice that I would give to all women who homeschool is to greet your husband with a happy face each evening.

I'm not saying you should "fake it till you make it". We all have days when the last thing we want to do is muster up a super-bubbly personality over the dinner table! But even on the hardest homeschool day we can offer a smile as our beloved comes home.

I cannot express how important this one act is. A sweet smile, a warm embrace, a kiss on the cheek and you've set the tone for the entire evening. On our really, really terrific days we can do this with ease. On our average days, it will take a little more effort. Now on those long and exhausting days, you may not be feeling it, but ask the Lord to help you welcome your husband home with genuine affection. Over time it will feel unnatural to be "grouchy" at the end of the day. And your husband will likely become happier overall as well.

This is hard to write, because I have in no way mastered it. But by the grace of God I will grow in this area. I am certain you will, too.

Proverbs 16:1 – To humans belong the plans of the heart, but from the Lord comes the proper answer of the tongue.

Sometimes the right answer really is not the right answer. I'm sure you have experienced this, as have I. Sometimes your child may need to know that you believe in her more than she needs to know the correct answer to her math problem.

Often we have put so much into the planning process of homeschooling that we miss out on the opportunity to "be there" for our children. Rely on the Lord to give the real "right answer" and our kids will grow in their walk with Him along with their academic growth.

Always be open to the Lord's version of the right answer and not only will you success in educating your children, you will have established a loving relationship with them as well. And that is of far, far greater worth.

Make record keeping a priority and you will save yourself much heartache later on.

It's far too easy to put away the textbooks at the end of the homeschool day and not properly document each child's work. The problem, however, is that today's ease becomes tomorrow's headache.

Whether you live in a state that requires plenteous documentation or none at all, you really do need to make record keeping a priority. Preparing transcripts, comparing and contrasting curriculum, and ensuring each subsequent homeschool year is not a "repeat"all demand good records. For you and for your children, this is very important.

My advice? Grade daily – do not put it off! And be specific in your planner or grade book. Rather than: *"Julia – math- 96%"* write *"Julia – grade 6 – Saxon 7/6 – lesson #54 – 96%".* This is the best way to make your future planning and GPA calculating easy!

I have learned this lesson the hard way. Delaying grading, keeping vague records and forgetting who read which book when all caught up with me at one time or another. Good record-keeping will pay you back in spades!

Week Five, Day 3

Hebrews 5:14 – Solid food is for the mature, who by constant use have trained themselves to distinguish good from evil.

This verse reminds me that becoming mature in Christ is a process, and that I absolutely must be a part of that process. It teaches that I will be trained by constant use. And it clearly states that I will be able to distinguish good from evil by that constant use.

And the opposite is also true: when I neglect the constant use of all I have learned and have available to me through God's Word, then I will not be able to distinguish good from evil. I will be unable to handle solid food – good, mature, Biblical teaching – because I have behaved childishly and neglected training that leads to maturity.

How many problems could be prevented if I would train myself the way Hebrews tells me to? How would my children benefit from mature training? Would our churches be filled with healthier Christians? Could our neighborhoods be transformed? Would the lost see something real, such as actual change that would draw them to Christ?

Is it possible that a large part of our current problem within our families and churches is a maturity problem? Let's be mature and begin to influence others through that maturity. And the huge blessing of distinguishing good from evil, of avoiding the enemy's deceptions and schemes, will be our daily blessing to enjoy.

Week Five, Day 4

"The secret of walking closely with Christ, and working successfully for Him, is to fully realize that we are His beloved." – A.B. Simpson

When we do not really grasp how dearly God loves us, it becomes almost impossible to be successful as we do the work He has called us to. We can probably do a pretty decent job, mustering up our strength and putting our shoulder to the plow. But we won't be walking closely with our Lord, and our relationship with our Father is the true measure of our success.

One practice that is particularly beneficial is to sit quietly before the Lord, asking Him to fill you with a sure knowledge of His great love. This may take some time and may feel strange at first, but if you will try it for a few days, I believe you will be changed as He begins to reveal to you how great His love for you really is.

Set aside time, beginning today, to get alone with the Father and let Him show you the love He has for you. You will find so much more success in your daily tasks and so much more delight in the people you do life with when you are filled with His love.

Week Five, Day 5

<u>Proverbs 15:33b</u> – and humility comes before honor.

Homeschool families tend to endure a lot of questioning – from family, neighbors, friends, even total strangers! It is often a frustrating experience! After all, what gives all these folks the right to think they can ask such personal, and often offensive, questions?

I have found that in due time my "questioners" were indeed silenced. As my children got older, began to graduate and head off to college, run their own small businesses during their high school years, those who spoke the most sharply about the detrimental aspects of homeschooling suddenly just…stopped…talking.

And interestingly, it has often been the children of those who so opposed homeschooling that have fallen into dire circumstances, in spite of their confidence that they had chosen the one correct way to educate their children and prepare them for life.

Be patient, homeschooling mother. Keep doing what the Father called you to do. Remain humble, even when people say things that are flat-out rude. God's Word is true. Your time of honor is on its way.

Week Six, Day 1

<u>1 John 3:4b</u> - in fact, sin is lawlessness.

John's letters to the church are truly remarkable. With abounding love, the disciple whom Jesus loved clearly lays out New Testament truths. Without mincing words, he allays any excuses for sin. And he always maintains his love for Christ's church.

In 1 John 3:4, he tells us that sin is, in plain and simple terms, lawlessness. Of course all of the Old Testament points out that where we fail to keep the law, there is sin. But John is writing to believers, to Christ-followers, not to the Jewish populace. So what does this verse mean for us?

In a nutshell, it tells us what sin is at its core, at its most base level.

Lawlessness is a refusal to be controlled by the law, being unbridled and unruly, a state of being in direct opposition to God. Rebellion. This is lawlessness. This is sin.

Having a working definition of what sin *is* gives us light for our path and brings clarity.

Don't we already understand lawlessness? Yes, indeed we do. While we may want to intellectualize or argue away the term "sin", we understand the lack of order, or lawlessness, quite well.

Don't excuse your sin. Simply call it what it is, repent, and accept the forgiveness that Jesus offers. Truly, His love endures forever.

Week Six, Day 2

Romans 9:16 – It does not, therefore, depend on human desire or effort but on God's mercy.

"Finish that math assignment."

"Rewrite this paper in MLA format."

"Fill in all the answers on your science review – even if it is repetitive."

And so it goes. We give instruction, cajole and correct, lecture and sigh…all in attempts to get the best result possible from our homeschooled children. None of this is wrong; often it is a necessary part of a homeschooling mother's job. Holding our children accountable for their academic work is the right thing to do.

But when we take too much of the burden of responsibility from God and place it squarely upon our own shoulders, we begin to depend on human effort rather than on God.

It's a balancing act to determine our role without moving into God's role. It requires much prayer and continual reliance upon the Lord to know when it's enough and when it's too much.

We can trust God to reveal when we are bearing His burdens, and we must trust Him to accomplish His will in our children's lives. Let your homeschool depend on God's mercy today.

Whatever may be going on in your life as a homeschooler, do not skip out on church attendance. The consequences are serious and severe if you do.

Attending a local church and being dialed-in, so to speak, is key to the long-term success of a Christian homeschool. Avoiding church, and thus avoiding relationships with other believers, is a dangerous path. It only leads to misery and potentially to ruin.

One reason why homeschool families need to make church attendance a priority is simply because the devil delights in getting us alone and isolated. Like a well-trained Army sniper, he can easily pick us off when we are alone. In greater number, however, he does not have the same effectiveness.

A second reason we need to be in fellowship in the local body of Christ is to keep us growing. From the worship to the sermon, prayer time to Sunday school, we grow. If you are not at church, you will miss out and your spiritual growth will be stunted.

Lastly, we need to be sharpened and to sharpen others. Yes, this will most certainly lead to questions and perhaps even conflict regarding your family's decision to homeschool. But years of experience have taught me that this is exactly the type of growth I need. It is alright to answer someone's questions about homeschooling, and so sharpen their understanding about that choice. It's best for the body as a whole to see what Christian homeschooling really is.

Don't neglect regular church attendance; it's vital for your well-being.

Week Six, Day 4

Isaiah 12:3 – With joy you will draw water from the wells of salvation.

It is far too easy to lose our joy due to the daily grind of homeschooling. At times we fool ourselves into thinking that we are really only lacking joy due to the season of life we are in. But I promise you, that is simply not true. From the first waves of morning sickness with your first child, to the moment your youngest graduates, there is no end to the seasons that can be joy stealers. Don't succumb to this tactic of the enemy. Be willing to fight those feelings of heaviness and push into joy, drawn from Jesus at the well of salvation.

If the joy of the Lord truly is your strength, then it only makes sense that the enemy will steal your joy if he aims to steal your strength. Once you recognize this scheme, be sure to take a firm stand against it. Your joy in the Lord is a powerful weapon, a choice gift bestowed upon you by your loving Father. Use your weapon well, fight with it every single day. Be joyful always!

Awaken with a thankful, joyful heart. Reset your attitude to one of joy as many times as you need to throughout the day. Keep a joyful journal and document things that bless you. Choose to smile rather than to scowl. Be joyful, and watch the enemy lose ground in your life.

I will say it again, be joyful always. Be joyful today.

Week Six, Day 5

John 12:43 – for they loved human praise more than praise from God.

Overall, homeschoolers are pretty well prepared to be viewed as odd ducks. As much as homeschooling has grown and is now seen as a valid educational option, it is still not the norm. So it stands to reason that homeschoolers, as a whole, don't love the approval of men…right?

For the most part, this is probably true. But there may still be a group of people whose attention and approval we find ourselves vying for. Yours maybe different than mine, but in the end it doesn't really matter whose approval we are seeking. It's all wrong, unless of course it's God's approval we seek.

Examples of those we desire to please may include our parents, pastors, our spouse, siblings, former co-workers, neighbors, your spouse's co-workers or friends, even others within the homeschool community. Nip this in the bud. *Always* nip it in the bud! It is a monster that will lurk around at all times, so push back against it and recommit your homeschool to the Lord alone.

Continually ask Him to show you that only His approval matters.

Week Seven, Day 1

"We are Christians. This should be plain for all folks to see, whether we speak or be silent." – Alexander McLaren

If you are a Christian woman, then it should be apparent to those looking on that you are such. If people have known you for awhile and do not know that Jesus has your heart, then perhaps He does not have as much of your heart as you believe He does. We do not need to turn the world into investigative reporters before our Christianity is made known. They should know it by the way we live. We ought to be different.

Starting with your daily homeschool routine, and moving into every other aspect of your life, pray and ask the Lord to make His presence visible through you. He desires to be known, and to be made real to others, through each of His children. Don't hide Him away. Let Him make you into the very best you that you can be. And let others see it!

God is glorified when we let Him be glorified – He is made known as we allow Him to be known through us.

A lost and hurting world sees what you are, and what you are not. Be the you that Jesus wants you to be today.

Week Seven, Day 2

Malachi 3:6a – "I the Lord do not change."

God does not change. He has not ever changed. Nor will He ever change. He is the Lord and He changes not.

If we compromise with the world, and succumb to its lures, we must do so with the full knowledge that our God does not, cannot, and will not change, and by cleaving to the world we cause Him great grief as we walk in unholiness.

There is no draw that the world offers which will ever deliver what we hope it will. Hoping that the world will one day give us any real fulfillment is the truest form of wishful thinking. And it is futile.

Our Lord does not change. And that is what makes Him the only safe place we can run to. Let His unchangeable nature be the thing that draws you away from the world. Be drawn straight into His loving arms.

Week Seven, Day 3

Phillipians 1:27a – Whatever happens, conduct yourselves in a manner worthy of the gospel of Christ.

If you are not a mother who homeschools it is probably nearly impossible to imagine how difficult it can be for a homeschooling mother to maintain a level of calm on a continuing basis. In fact, without the power of the Lord, I would venture to say it is impossible.

This verse, Phillipians 1:27, reminds me once again that I cannot live the Christian life in my own strength. Actually, I cannot do anything in a godly manner in my own strength. Truly to do things in my own strength trips me up and harms others!

For me to conduct myself in a manner worthy of the gospel of Christ, I must allow the Holy Spirit to do His work in me as well through me. And only when I yield fully to Him am I able to conduct myself in a worthy manner.

The same is true for you. Let's all yield to the Lord. Let's all be worthy of Christ's gospel in our conduct. Let's do it today.

Week Seven, Day 4

<u>Hebrews 4:12</u> – For the word of God is alive and active. Sharper than any double-edged sword, it penetrates even to dividing soul and spirit, joints and marrow; it judges the thoughts and attitudes of the heart.

For any problem which you might have, the Bible holds the answer. Any struggle your child may face, the Bible holds the answer. No matter the circumstance, the answer is available to you. It is not hidden away, locked up and shrouded in mystery. It is not difficult to obtain. God is not holding out on you.

Hebrews 4:12 teaches us that God's Word is anything but a stagnant, aged book. It is living and active. It will be active in your life to the degree you allow it access. The sharp sword of the Word truly does separate all those confusing things that cause discouragement. It will reveal bad – and good! – attitudes. It judges the thoughts that do not align with the truth, and it judges your true intent in ways mere man cannot.

The Word of God does exactly what God intends it to do. No portion of His plans ever fail. His Word does not return to Him void.

Let the Word speak to your problem areas. Do not seek the world's wisdom, which is faulty at best and detrimental and destructive at worst. God's Word is designed to do the delicate work of dividing bone and marrow. Don't attempt to do in the flesh what can only be done in the Spirit.

Find true refreshment by letting God's Word do what it was designed to do. Then be prepared for the peace of God to guard your heart.

Week Seven, Day 5

Psalm 25:5a – Guide me in your truth and teach me.

Homeschooling mothers have to learn how to teach every subject to multiple ages, often on the fly with a toddler attached to the hip!

It's normal to feel overwhelmed and under-qualified at times. And it can be hard not to succumb to fear when we begin to feel inadequate.

But there is a solution! Psalm 25:5 asks God to guide us in His truth. It is a prayer asking Him to teach us.

Indeed, asking God to make us fit to teach is truly the only answer to inadequacy. And He is the All-Sufficient One. Trust Him as you pray for His truth to be your teacher and your guide.

<u>Proverbs 30:1b</u> – I am weary, God, but I can prevail.

This verse describes exactly what motherhood and homeschooling can feel like.

Isn't it a comfort to know that God understands how wearying life can be? He understands the daily wearing out that mothers experience. He gets it. Truly, He understands it all.

There is no situation, good or bad, for which God's Word does not hold the answer. It's all there, all that you need for every moment of every day of your life. But it will remain elusive to you if you don't spend time reading the Bible.

Life is going to make us weary. It is unavoidable. But we can prevail if we use the tools the Lord has provided. Remember that you do not need to live the homeschool life in your own strength. Instead, accept the fact that you can only prevail by relying completely upon the Lord.

Let His Word be your guide throughout all aspects of life. Open your Bible and see for yourself how God will meet you in your weariness.

Luke 14:28 – "Suppose one of you wants to build a tower. Won't you first sit down and estimate the cost to see if you have enough money to complete it?"

Count the cost.

You have surely heard that saying, and most likely you can attribute it to Jesus' words in Luke 14:28. But have you ever applied it to each of your children's education?

I have five children. That means each child is one-fifth of my primary ministry. Now that I have two in college, my ministry in the homeschooling sense has changed. Come next fall, when three of our children will be in college, my two daughters still at home will each become one-half of my homeschool ministry. So my ministry has changed along with my season of life.

Where are you on this path right now? Assign each child a percentage of your "ministry" and then raise them, educate them, with that percentage in mind.

You will find it easier to make decisions regarding curriculum and activities for each child, and your job as a homeschooler will become easier as you remember that each one of your children is a key part of the largest ministry the Lord has given you.

Week Eight, Day 3

Luke 1:37 – For no word of God will ever fail.

Have you ever taken hold of one of God's promises and made it your own? If you haven't, can I encourage you to seek a promise from the Lord and then stand upon it firmly? There is nothing quite like experiencing first-hand the thrill of seeing the Lord keep His promises to you.

If all God's promises prove true – and they do! – and we have access to His promises in the Word – and we do! – then doesn't it stand to reason we ought to live believing those promises? Often the only thing that stands in our way is, well, us.

God does not lie, God does not change, no Word of His will ever fail. We, however, do lie, do change, and do fail. But in spite of our shortcomings, we are fully able to take God at His Word. And His Word says it will never fail.

If you struggle believing that He has specific promises that are just for you, start small. Pray that the Lord will reveal a promise to you as you read the Bible and when He does, memorize it. Remind yourself of it – often! Several times each day. And then watch God keep His promise to you.

Keep moving on to bigger and better promises. He will change your life as you trust Him more. And in this, He will not fail.

Week Eight, Day 4

<u>Proverbs 4:23</u> – Above all else, guard your heart, for everything you do flows from it.

It is easy for discouragement to settle into an unguarded heart. Discontent, unforgiveness, anger, bitterness, doubt – these all find themselves readily at home in a heart which has its guard down. Truly, if you are angry, if you are bitter, if you are afraid, it flows from your heart that is not closely guarded.

So what does a well-guarded heart look like? It is represented by a life of peace, of love, contentment, forgiveness, and all the other characteristics that are commonly known as the fruit of the Spirit. When the things flowing out of you are aligned with New Testament Christianity, your heart most likely has a guard over it.

We guard our hearts by choosing wisely who and what we listen to, what we read and watch (television, movies, or our smart phones), who our close friendships are with, and perhaps above all, what we think. When the Holy Spirit governs our minds and our hearts, we have Him as our mighty heart-guard.

Be aware of what flows out of your heart, because it is a sure-fire way to know how well your heart is being guarded.

Week Eight, Day 5

Isaiah 41:10c – I will strengthen you…

Four words that form a fragment of a sentence. But what a powerful punch they pack

He will strengthen you. He will strengthen me. We will be strengthened. He says so.

His strength never runs out, so we can all go from strength to strength. It's a new supply for us, all day, every day, as often as we need it. And His faithfulness, His strength, His great love, endures for all generations. So there is plenty to go around for you, for your children, for your grandchildren…for all who will receive Him. There is plenty.

Ask Him for strength today, and He will give all that you need. Remember, however, that does not mean all that you *want*. Because sometimes He gives us just enough strength to keep us close to Him, continually depending on Him and drawing us near.

The strength you need today is promised to you. And He always keeps His promises.

Week Nine, Day 1

Good things come from the Lord, according to James 1:17. In fact, this truth is affirmed again and again all throughout the Bible.

My question for you today is this: Are you receiving, openly, all the good things God has for you?

One of the biggest problems of our day is, as mothers, we have a very difficult time receiving good things without an equal measure guilt.

Perhaps we're so conflicted that while we live in such an over-the-top, affluent society, we know how Christians all around the world live, and so we cannot joyfully and thankfully accept good things.

But God truly does have good for each of us, and He wants us to receive it without guilt.

I don't mean piles of money, luxury vacations on cruise ships in the Caribbean, and the like. I simply mean whatever "good things" He has for us, we should accept without any guilt or shame. And knowing that it's okay to enjoy what God has given us, to actually enjoy our lives, opens our hearts to praise Him in a whole new way.

Proverbs 12:4a – A wife of noble character is her husband's crown.

Don't allow yourself to become so engrossed in homeschooling that your fail to remember that before you were a mom, before you were a homeschooler, first you were one man's wife.

You cannot be of noble character and be neglectful of your husband. This is a non-negotiable fact. An attentive wife goes hand-in-hand with a woman of noble character.

So in whatever areas you suspect you have been neglecting your spouse, get it right with God and then get it right in your daily life.

You don't need me to tell you how to fix whatever it is that needs fixing. Even if you think you need me tell you...trust me, you don't. The Holy Spirit will tell you if you but ask. Your husband will tell you, if he believes you really want an honest answer. Your heart, while deceitful above all things, will tell you.

Just submit to the Lord, be a blessing to your husband, and watch yourself become his crown.

Week Nine, Day 3

Do you have a dream? Maybe a simple dream, like an organized kitchen. Perhaps a complex dream, like a ministry to the homeless in your community.

Did you ever consider that if you don't take the time to entrust your dream to God it may never come to fruition?

I'm not saying hard work cannot make your dream come true. There are plenty of examples that you can get something done without committing it to God. But the Word promises that when we commit our plans to the Lord, they will succeed.

I don't want to have unfulfilled dreams that the Lord would love to fulfill. So I choose to continually recommit my dreams to Him. And then I trust Him. And I have great peace. I grow closer to Him. It truly is a win-win.

Give your dreams to your loving Father. Trust fully in Him. Live a life that is a dream come true.

Week Nine, Day 4

Colossians 3:16 – Let the message of Christ dwell in you richly as you teach and admonish one another....

Every subject can be taught with a focus on Christ. Not only daily devotions and Bible lessons, but even math and grammar.

Be creative in trying new ways to incorporate God's Word and Biblical truths. Talk about the Lord all throughout the school day. And perhaps most important of all, let the Word dwell in you, the mom in your family's homeschool.

As the mother, your attitude sets the tone for the entire family. When the Word of God is dwelling in you richly (as in abundantly, overflowing and gushing out of you) then you will find it relatively easy to add God's Word to every school subject. A level of calm will overtake your home, and you will walk in blessings untold.

A stressed out mom will torpedo a happy homeschool every time.

"Are you where God would have you to be? If not, come out, and at once, for you certainly ought not to be there. If you are, then be afraid to complain of circumstances which God has ordained on purpose to work out in you the very image and likeness of His Son." – Mark Guy Pearse

Do you homeschool because it is God's call on your life? This isn't the only reason to homeschool, but if it happens to be the reason for your homeschool, then you need to do your work without an attitude. There should be no room for complaining in doing God's will. If there is a sour attitude, then it is time to invest in a season of prayer. Perhaps the work you are doing needs to change, or perhaps just your bad attitude.

Homeschooling is too large an endeavor to do begrudgingly. Mom's attitude is contagious, and it will be caught by the children. Even your spouse will begin to change if you maintain a consistently negative mood.

Resetting your attitude can be as simple as reminding yourself why you began homeschooling in the first place. And if it was God's call that led you here, then be sure to align your attitude with His will for your life.

Therein lie the greatest blessings, and trust me, those are too valuable to miss out on.

Week Ten, Day 1

Psalm 1:1 – Blessed is the one who does not walk in step with the wicked or stand in the way that sinners take or sit in the company of mockers.

I have a quick prayer that I ask of the Lord almost every morning, based on Psalm 1, verse 1. I simply pray that on that particular day, He would prevent me from walking in the path of sinners, from sitting in the seat of mockers, and from having ungodly counsel of any sort. Simple, right? And yet very powerful.

It is so easy to walk in step with the wicked and not even know I am doing so. Maybe I think something negative about another person, and then I share that thought aloud with someone else. In my life, that constitutes walking in step with the wicked.

Or maybe I make jokes at someone else's expense. Even if I do not intend to be hurtful, being a mocker of any sort is against God's good and perfect and pleasing will. He loves all those He has created, and who am I to say a mocking word about those that He so dearly loves? Jesus truly did die for the sin of all mankind, and when I ask Him to keep me from a mocking attitude, He reminds me of His death borne out of love.

Asking the Lord to keep me from ungodly counsel of any sort, just for today, has been one of the mightiest prayers I have learned to pray. I find that everything I do is impacted by this prayer for covering and wisdom, from impulse purchases to impatience with my children. I used to think that ungodly counsel was simply receiving advice from those who do not walk in the Lord's ways. However, I have learned that ungodly counsel comes from sources which I hadn't been guarding against. I highly encourage you to ask the Lord to keep you from ungodly counsel today; it has been a life-changing exercise for me!

Be blessed today as you see to walk with the Lord alone.

It has been said that the men who move the world are those who do not let the world move them. I would add that a woman, a mother, who does not let the world move her in her own home will one day move the world through her children.

Raising up children who love the Lord is among the most noble and highest callings available to mankind. It is not for the faint of heart, and no slouch can truly complete this task. It requires a woman who is completely sold out to the Lord, who depends upon Him moment by moment, day by day.

Being a mother who homeschools does not automatically guard your children from temptation and hardship. Nor does is ensure that your children will all love and serve the Lord. But it is a means of abundant opportunity, as we daily have the time afforded us to pray over them and teach them from God's Word. Any other educational option removes them from the home. Homeschooling gives us far more direct contact with our children. We ought to use that time wisely, investing it as a precious commodity.

You can be a mother who moves the world through her children by not being a woman who is moved by the world.

Week Ten, Day 3

<u>1 Corinthians 12:3b</u> – no one can say, "Jesus is Lord" except by the Holy Spirit.

Do you have friends or family that do not know Jesus as Lord and Savior? Most of us do, and at times we can become overwhelmed with the understanding of the eternal consequences of their spiritual condition. It is painful to think about, but it is also important that we remain in prayer for our loved ones.

Consider praying 1 Corinthians 12:3 for those who do not know the Lord personally, asking the Holy Spirit to woo them and draw them to an understanding of Who Jesus is. Seek Him to reveal their need of a Savior. Pray this often and in love.

After all, if no one can say "Jesus is Lord" except by the Holy Spirit, then can there be any better way to pray for our lost loved ones than by asking the Holy Spirit to make this truth known?

Do not grow weary. Keep praying and believe you will one day see results. This is one prayer that God truly loves to answer, as He has revealed in His Word that He desires none should perish, but that all should come to a knowledge of the truth. Continue in prayer today.

Week Ten, Day 4

Titus 2:10 – so that in every way they will make the teaching about God our Savior attractive.

Can you think of a better goal in your homeschool than to make teaching about the Savior attractive to your children? Even as we raise our children in Christian homes, we should be aware of making the gospel attractive to them.

I cannot give you a prescribed formula for applying this verse work in your homeschool. Each child is unique and as parents we need to find means of teaching Biblical truths that are not unattractive to them.

Remember what has touched your heart throughout your walk with the Lord. Was it not, at one time one thing, and later on something quite different? Our children are much the same. One Bible lesson or curriculum may not speak to them all in the same manner at the same age. Be aware that Titus 2 encourages us to keep making the gospel attractive by the way we live in addition to our curriculum choices. And of course, keep family devotions with Bible reading as a key part of your family life. You cannot go wrong reading directly from God's Word.

Be continually open to the Holy Spirit, asking Him to teach you how to teach about Him in ways that attract the hearts of your children.

Week Ten, Day 5

"The life of faith is a life of obedience." – Andrew Murray

Ah, that word "obedience". Nine letters that can cause so much discomfort. Obedience. So simple and yet so difficult.

Like it or not, an obedient life is one that reflects the Lord to a lost and hurting world. A disobedient heart speaks the lie that God is not trustworthy or true.

To be an accurate reflection of Jesus, I must live an obedient life. There is a zero percent chance of properly reflecting God if I am disobeying Him. No chance at all. Who wants that to be their life legacy?

Become an obedient woman today. Do not wait, do not put it off. Whatever it is that He has told you to do, do it. Immediately. And if you think you're already pretty obedient, then be sure to thank Him for enabling you to quickly obey. Be brave enough to ask Him to show you where you might not be obeying. If there is an area of disobedience, He will reveal it to you.

Obedience is the mark of a life lived for Him and it makes for a beautiful reflection.

Week Eleven, Day 1

Psalm 119:50b – Your promise renews my life.

May I be very candid and share from my heart a few things that I have learned the hard way?

Having the day all to myself does not renew me. Taking a wonderful family vacation does not renew me (although the memories made on vacation do bless me!). Having a larger income does not renew me. Losing a fair amount of weight and being "thinner" has not renewed me.

The way that my heart, my life, is renewed is by enjoying the presence of the Lord, by fostering my relationship with Him, by hearing His promises to me and resting on them.

I can say with total certainty that you will only be truly renewed in the same manner. Expect Jesus to be your everything, your all in all today, and He surely will be.

His renewal is the only one that lasts, that counts for eternity, that is real. Let the great Renewer do His work in you today.

Week Eleven, Day 2

"There is something infinitely better than doing a great thing for God, and the infinitely better thing is to be where God wants us to be, to do what God wants us to do, and to have no will apart from His." – G. Campbell Morgan

Homeschooling is a long road. It is always tempting to consider giving up when a task is so long in the doing. But what benefit ever comes from quitting? What great gain can there be from taking a break or stopping altogether?

Homeschooling may not seem to be the "big thing" you desire to do for God. It may be tempting to consider setting it aside for some greater work for the kingdom. But choose carefully, consider wisely, whether that is actually the truth. It is always best to be where God wants you, doing something that is slow and steady, than to be outside of His will doing some seemingly greater thing.

Have no will regarding your life's work apart from His will.

Week Eleven, Day 3

There is only so much time in a day and the time spent on smart phones or the internet is usually, well, wasted time.

For me, the key has been to have set times to check email or text messages or Facebook. Anything not homeschool related (or essential to my family's well-being) must be set aside or homeschooling and other essentials will be shoved aside. I can put my Blackberry in another room during school hours. If my husband sends a text and I don't reply quickly, he calls the home phone. I haven't missed out on anything of vital importance by leaving my phone in the other room during the school day.

I also make it a point to look my children in the eye whenever they are speaking to me. At times more than one child is talking at once, which makes it a little tricky to provide my undivided attention, but that is part of having a large family!

If you were to ask me why I do these things, I would tell you it is because the Lord convicted me that too much time with a PC on is not so different then sending my children to public school. In fact, it may be worse based on the sadness I have seen on their faces when my smart phone has pulled me away when they needed me close.

Time is fleeting. It needs to be spent wisely. Invest your time in your family today.

Week Eleven, Day 4

What do you dislike most about homeschooling?

If we are honest, many of us have at least one thing about homeschooling that we really cannot stand. For many years, I truly despised daily grading. It was always looming there, in a gigantic pile, waiting for me. Every single day! So many evenings spent grading, feeling as if I were missing out on family time or failing to complete other tasks around the house. The homeschool day is not finished until I have graded every single subject for every single child and recorded every single detail in my planner. It's just no fun! Just like the laundry, it never goes away.

But one day it will go away. In fact, it already has for my two children who are in college. My middle daughter graduates this year and next year my two youngest will be a senior and a sophomore. My greatest homeschool burden is disappearing before my very eyes…and it isn't a joyful thing!

Now I find that when I receive a text from one of my college kids asking me to look over a paper, I don't mind so much. Even if I am out of the house running errands and end up reading the document on my Blackberry, I am sure to do it right away and not put it off. Why? Because it is a reminder that the homeschool years fly by far too quickly.

As I have allowed the Lord to show me how fleeting the time truly is, He has changed my heart and I can say I no longer despise grading. In fact, I may even enjoy it…just a little bit.

Romans 14:23b – and everything that does not come from faith is sin.

The Bible has no shortage of "hard teachings" (see John 6:60). Read for a short while and there will be something that challenges your way of thinking. I would even go so far as to say that if your thinking has not been challenged by what the Bible says, you have probably not read enough of it.

Romans 14:23 poses a very hard teaching. In no uncertain terms it tells us that everything which does not come from faith is sin. *Every-single-thing*.

First, it helps to define what is meant by "faith". We will be frustrated if we have faith in our own faith, attempting to muster up more and more of it in our own strength. However, when we place our faith solely in God and humbly ask Him to increase our faith, then that is true faith.

So, Romans 14:23 seems to be teaching us that anything, and everything, that does not come from our securely based faith in Christ alone, is sin. What in your life, your homeschool, your relationships is sin by this qualifier? Yes, this is a very hard teaching. But in its hard truth, we find a path toward Christ-likeness. Let the Word be your personal refining fire and let Him be the source of your faith.

Week Twelve, Day 1

    Hebrews 3:13 – But encourage one another daily, as long as it is called 'Today', so that none of you may be hardened by sin's deceitfulness.

    Your children are not only your offspring, they are also members of the body of Christ. We don't always remember to treat them as such. But at times, that is exactly what is missing in our relationships with our children.

    You have today, this very moment, to be an encourager. To remind them that Jesus' words are true. That this life is fleeting and that one day we will be in eternity with our Lord. Today you can encourage them in the hope that they will not be hardened by sin's deceitfulness.

    Make sure that as long as it is called 'Today', you are in their corner cheering them on in their personal relationships with Jesus. Spur them on as they keep their hearts close to Him, soft and tender and unhardened by the sneakiness of sin. This ought to be a primary goal as homeschooling mothers. Be an encourager today.

Week Twelve, Day 2

<u>Isaiah 34:17a</u> – He allots their portions…

Your allotment in life, of all things good or bad, is not outside of the Lord's mighty right hand. Not one hardship or one blessing is beyond Him. He allots us our portions.

It is easier by far to gripe about the hand life has dealt us than to accept it all from God's hand. Isn't that the opposite of a grateful heart and a content attitude? It also is an indicator of a lack of trust in God. As believers, we must move beyond this lack of trust. Failure to grow in our ability to trust God fully is in reality sin. James 4:17 teaches that if anyone knows the good they ought to do and fails to do it, then that is sin. Surely trusting God more and more is something very good that we all ought to do. Therefore failure to trust Him more and more is sinful.

My portion, the whole of it, has been allotted to me by my good, loving, generous God. I must choose to thank Him for all He has allotted to me, for in any other behavior I am failing to honor Him.

Enjoy your allotment today. It comes to you straight from the hand of your Father.

Week Twelve, Day 3

Save time so you don't waste time.

Take a menu plan as an example. Implemented properly, it can eliminate huge amounts of stress and save loads of time for a homeschooling mother. The time spent preparing menus, grocery shopping, and doing some prep work in the kitchen is worth it because the weeks when we use a menu plan run so much more smoothly than the weeks when we choose to wing it instead.

Apply this principle to other areas in your home and see what happens. Take laundry, for instance. Make a plan and stick with it, for one entire week. See if it reduces your mom stress, and if your kids will be better prepared by having any sports uniforms washed ahead of time rather than at the last minute. Your husband may be pleased with the result.

Maybe you are too overwhelmed to have a plan for every single area of your life, but could you try out a couple of plans for some key problem areas and see how it goes? You may find that you actually like living a low-stress life!

Week Twelve, Day 4

Job 14:17 – My offenses will be sealed up in a bag; you will cover over my sin.

I love this quote from the book of Job. It is penned from a heart filled with grief and despair. Yet that heavy heart continued to take hold of the goodness of the Lord, even in between suffocating waves of agonizing mourning.

What a life lesson we can learn from Job! We will all endure tragedy, we will surely all grieve in this life. But we will not all recall that our God comforts us, guides us and most amazingly of all, covers over all our sin.

That covering-over love was what took Jesus to the cross. That covering-over love is what draws us to Him. That covering-over love is what will comfort us in our grief and will spill over to others in theirs.

Thank You, Father, for Your unending love that covers over so, so much in my life.

Week Twelve, Day 5

What is most important to you?

Once you have identified the most important things for your homeschool, your family, your marriage, and so on, write them down. Then write down the things you do regularly, on a daily or weekly basis. Things that take up the bulk of your time.

Does your use of time reflect your priorities? If yes, terrific! You are probably a very balanced person!

If no, take a look at those things that fill your time. Do a double-take at that list of priorities. What is out of whack?

Reevaluate both your priorities and your daily activities alongside your husband, seeking his advice and looking at your schedule through a fresh set of eyes. Be brave enough to make the changes that are necessary in order to align your life with your goals. Don't be afraid of this crucial step! After all, you only live once and God has given you the task of homeschooling your particular children at this particular season of your one-and-only life.

In light of that reality, it isn't so hard to make a few changes. Find out where your time goes, and then make it go where it ought to be going.

Week Thirteen, Day 1

We all want an answer to the age-old question, "Why am I here?" Philippians 3:10 holds part of the answer. In the New Living Translation it reads, "I want to know Christ and experience the mighty power that raised him from the dead.

I'm not here to amass a fortune, become famous or make a name for myself. Conversely, I'm not here to become a wallflower, fade in anonymity or loathe myself. I am here to glorify God. I do that first by knowing Christ. My children are here for the same purpose.

If He is truly our all in all, then we need to live as if we believe it. Ask the Lord to help you know Him more and more and more, every single day. Pray that He will allow you to experience the mighty power that raised Him from the dead. You will discover the answer to the question, "Why am I here?"

All of your life, including your role as a homeschooling mother, will be blessed as you continue to know Christ more and more. Know Him today, and then make Him known.

<u>2 Corinthians 3:17</u> – Now the Lord is Spirit, and where the Spirit of the Lord is, there is freedom.

Are you living your life like a woman who is free? Or are you finding yourself in bondage, enslaved, living under the heavy burden of the law? As a woman who has been homeschooling her children for nearly two decades, I can testify that it is actually very easy to become caught up in attitudes and homeschool circles that cause us to live under the law rather than in the freedom which Christ has for us.

Curriculum, co-ops, culture, and insecurity all push us to live under the law. Do this; don't do that. Eat this; don't eat that. Use this math program; avoid that history book. Read only this type of book for recreational reading, because if you read anything else you're not godly enough to be a good homeschooling mother.

Please do not misunderstand me here; there are certainly plenty of books that Christian women should never read! Anything that glorifies or justifies sin is not quality reading material. My desire is not to tell you that all boundaries are wrong, but rather to tell you that being Spirit-led is always right. The only way to keep from becoming burdened again by the law is to be a woman who is led by the Holy Spirit.

Christ has set us free. Have you applied that freedom to yourself? To your homeschool?

Week Thirteen, Day 3

Deuteronomy 33:25b – and your strength will equal your days.

Have you ever considered how old you will be when you finish homeschooling all of your children? It can seem like a very, very long set of years stretching far into the distance. Thinking about it usually makes you feel nothing short of exhausted!

Deuteronomy 33:25 states that our strength will match our days. We will have what we need for each day of our lives, come what may in the course of that day. That includes the many years of homeschooling. The caveat to this promise of strength is that we ought not focus on the many tomorrows yet to come. By exhausting today's grace as we focus on tomorrow's tasks, we leave ourselves open to discouragement and fatigue.

Don't fall into the trap of pondering the heavy load of all the many years to come. Rather, enjoy the grace afforded you today and choose to delight in each day as it comes.

His promise to give you strength equal to your days will prove true. So use today's strength for today.

Don't believe everything you hear.

Whether it's a description of a phonics program or the lure of the latest fad diet, half-truths and outright falsehoods are all around us.

Not every child will respond well to even the very best curriculum. And not all that we see and hear and read is true. Be careful not to set your expectations too high, whether with people or things. Be sure to pray and ask God, who knows all, to reveal what you need to know.

Do not live in fear that a dangerous lie is lurking around every corner. But don't live in "La-La Land" either, believing no one and nothing would ever deceive you.

Remember that not all deceit is intentional. That math program may have worked wonders for the mom who reviewed it on her blog. It simply may not be best for your family.

Most importantly, do not believe the lies that the enemy whispers to you. Reject all thoughts that do not align with God's Word. Let God's truth be the loudest thing you hear each day.

Week Thirteen, Day 5

Exodus 14:14 – The Lord Himself will fight for you. Just stay calm. (New Living Translation)

I will freely admit, as a homeschooling mother to five, there have been many occasions wherein I needed to remain calm and allow the Lord to fight for me….and indeed I flat-out panicked.

Perhaps you can relate! During a season of unemployment, or maybe due to an extended illness that left you stretched too thin. Or the day-to-day pressure that comes with homeschooling. It is far easier to give in to fret and fear than it is to actually trust in the Lord and His deliverance.

These words, "Just stay calm", tell us what our part in the process is. If you are focused on the problem at hand, you will not be able to remain calm. If you try and handle things in your own strength, you surely won't stay calm.

Yet if you trust in the Lord, allowing yourself to rest in Him, you will find yourself staying calm. It is truly miraculous for high-strung women like me!

After all, for believers, it isn't about the calm before the storm. It's all about the calm during the storm.

Week Fourteen, Day 1

2 Thessalonians 3:11-13 – We hear that some among you are idle and disruptive. They are not busy; they are busybodies. Such people we command and urge in the Lord Jesus Christ to settle down and earn the food they eat. And as for you, brothers and sisters, never tire of doing what is good.

When we are at home with our children so much of the time, it is really easy to do just the bare minimum, covering only the basics. Aren't homeschooling, errands, meals, laundry, survival chores that must be done, enough to keep a mom plenty busy? And yet, it may also leave us with just enough time to become busy-bodies. Perhaps, dare I say it, even a bit lazy.

I'm not advocating a work-a-holic mentality or a works-based Christianity. But I am suggesting a daily lifestyle that accepts the counsel and admonition of 2 Thessalonians chapter 3, where Paul tells us not to be idle, or a person who is disruptive and creates discord. We are not to be busybodies, but rather to be busy at home.

Here we are also told not to tire of what is good. Taking care of our homes and families most certainly qualifies as good, and so we should ask the Lord daily to help us not grow weary in it. He will strengthen us and He can take away any of our idle habits and busy-body natures.

Why not make this the homeschool year that transforms you from busybody to busy-mommy?

Week Fourteen, Day 2

1 Chronicles 4:40a – They found rich, good pasture, and the land was spacious, peaceful and quiet.

What a beautiful word picture is found in 1 Chronicles 4:40. I have found myself praying for lush pastures in a quiet and peaceful land. It is something we all seem to long for to one degree or another.

The Christian life comes with no guarantees. We are slaves to Christ, we have been bought with a price. While filled with blessings untold and joy unsearchable, there are many hard days in the life of a Christ follower. Knowing we cannot escape the struggles that come with life in a fallen world, may we still pray for the Lord's blessing and favor upon our homeschools, our marriages, our churches, our communities, and so on.

I do ask the Lord for lush pastures, for times of quiet and peace and refreshment. God has peaceful seasons for each of us. Even during high-stress times, He provides little pockets of peace and renewal. Keep asking Him to lead you to lush pastures. He is, after all, your Good Shepherd!

Week Fourteen, Day 3

<u>Daniel 12:4b</u> – Many will rush here and there, and knowledge will increase. (New Living Translation)

We have smart phones and tablets, which are even better than laptops, which were even better than PCs, which were even better than television, which was far better than radio, and that was of course better than the newspaper… On my Kindle I can carry a library of books. Satellite radio is available in my SUV, and I can listen to whatever type of music suits my fancy at the moment. My bills can be managed entirely online, so that I rarely need a stamp or a visit to the post office. On and on it goes.

What a tremendous increase in knowledge the last one-hundred and fifty years have brought! Daniel's vision of many rushing here and there surmises our generation's daily lifestyle.

What does it all mean for a Christian mother who home educates her children? I believe it means we are to beware! Be very aware! The end of time as we know it is drawing ever nearer; our focus must be on glorifying God. The increase of knowledge and the rushing about can easily pull our focus away from the reality the Jesus is indeed coming again.

Focus on Him today, and rather than rush about chaotically, rush into His arms.

George Mueller once said that we are very prone to want to answer our own prayers.

In what ways might this be true for us as homeschoolers? Do we wait patiently for the Lord to answer our prayers, or do we try to find a solution on our own?

Whether the problem is finding the right math curriculum, where our children should apply to college, or what to make for dinner, we can either trust God or we can take the DIY approach. He wants us to take every need to Him, and then to allow Him to answer in His own way and time.

George Mueller was said to have prayed about everything, from a lost key to confusing passages of Scripture. And of course he prayed for the daily needs of the hundreds of orphans in his care.

Think again about your desire to answer your own prayers. And think twice the next time you catch yourself doing it!

Week Fourteen, Day 5

Acts 20:23 – I only know that in every city the Holy Spirit warns me that prison and hardships are facing me.

Do you expect to hear from the Holy Spirit personally? On a daily basis?

If not, you need to adjust your expectations! Our Counselor, the Holy Spirit, is more willing to speak to us than we are to listen. What on earth might we hear from Him if we would but attune our ears?

In Acts 20:23, Paul states that he knew what was ahead because the Holy Spirit had warned him. He was not told to turn back, nor was he told to be afraid. Rather, Paul was prepared for what lie before him – simply because he expected to hear clearly from the Holy Spirit and was willing to accept what he was told, whether good or bad, without complaint.

Do you accept difficult news with the right attitude? Do you joyfully take good from the hand of the Lord, and angrily shove away bad? This is a poor way to respond. Reset your thinking in accordance with God's Word and willingly accept the Holy Spirit's instruction. Of course, that will never contradict the Bible. We shouldn't assume every thought that pops into our mind is from the Lord. When we do hear from Him, however, we ought to accept His will with open and obedient hearts.

Week Fifteen, Day 1

1 Corinthians 2:5 – so that your faith may not rest on human wisdom, but on God's power.

Never fall into the trap of thinking that your child's entire future rests on your shoulders. That is simply untrue! In a private or public school setting, no one person would be held responsible for a student's entire academic success, or failure. But we who homeschool put an enormous amount of pressure on ourselves in this regard.

Heaping loads of guilt-driven expectations upon ourselves is not the lifestyle God called us to. Heavy burdens that are self-imposed do not bring about the godly life that Christ desires. Burdens are burdensome; Jesus' yoke is light.

Yes, we are responsible for educating our children. I am an advocate of mother's doing the right thing for their children when it comes to home education. But we are not meant to do what only God can do. The end result will be due to His power, and for His glory.

We must submit to His leadership as we homeschool, knowing there will be plenty of hard work along the way. However our faith ought not rest on our own wisdom, but on God's power.

Week Fifteen, Day 2

Somewhere, I once read this quote: "Believing supplications are forecasts of the future."

It impacted me enough that I made note of it. And when I have re-read it, yet again it has impacted me.

My "rote" and repetitive prayers, which I can recite from memory, are not forecasts of anything, are they? My doubt-filled prayers are not going to help me accomplish anything for the kingdom of God.

Conversely, my believing prayers reach the ears, the heart, of my mighty, Almighty God. When He hears, He is moved. Moved to action.

That does not mean He is my giant sugar daddy in the sky. God is not a vending machine, doling out treats at our request. Those words are actually difficult for me to write, blasphemous as they are!

Indeed, I will not always "get" things exactly as I want them, even when I pray believing prayers with a proper attitude. But I will gain much more than I had imagined was possible.

Lay out a believing supplication before the Lord today, and watch for a beautiful forecast.

Week Fifteen, Day 3

Job 9:10 – He performs wonders that cannot be fathomed, miracles that cannot be counted.

If we can get ourselves to simply slow down a bit, we will find it much easier to be amazed at the things that God is doing right in our own homes.

Remember the delight you had when your child first began to read? Or when they played their first complete song on an instrument? Watching them develop those skills, were you in awe that the Lord was allowing you to participate in the process? There's no reason why every homeschool year shouldn't leave us in a bit of awe. We become so busy doing school that we easily forget the wonder of it all.

Don't let busy-ness steal the awesome things God is doing right out from under your nose. Remember to thank Him, to praise Him, for the wonders without measure He is doing in your family.

Week Fifteen, Day 4

<u>Matthew 6:14</u> – "For if you forgive other people when they sin against you, your heavenly Father will also forgive you."

A wealth of life-long, necessary truth lies here in the words of Jesus (Matt. 6:14). For the homeschooling mother, its truth spans the years spent living a lifestyle that is somewhat unique in our society. It holds the key to peace and opens the door to abundant grace…provided we actually do what it says to do.

There is an "if" in this verse, and that "if" carries quite a lot of weight. We must – *must* - forgive other people (as in any and all people) when they sin against us. Whatever that sin may be. Then, and only then, will our heavenly Father forgive us.

Jesus minces no words as He tells us that we must forgive in order to receive forgiveness.

The double blessing of this promise is that we free ourselves from the burdens of bitterness and revenge when we forgive. This is in addition to receiving the forgiveness of God for our own wrongs!

Be a woman who forgives. Do so out of love and obedience. And let your forgiveness be a lesson your homeschooled children will never forget. What a wonderful gift to give them!

Week Fifteen, Day 5

1 John 3:19 - ...we set our hearts at rest in his presence

You may be worn out from sleepless nights with a baby, early mornings with a toddler, long days of homeschooling and late nights catching up on dishes and laundry.

Your mind may be racing with a to-do list that far exceeds the hours in your day. The thought of writing lesson plans or teaching Algebra may cause you to want to hide in the bathroom all day long. Maybe you are expecting and morning-afternoon-all-day-long sickness leaves you unable to even think about making a wonderful dinner for your family this evening.

In all these circumstances, in any situation you face on any given day, you can set your heart at rest in His presence. I cannot come to your home and make dinner for your family tonight, but I can encourage you to enter into the Lord's presence and enjoy His perfect rest.

Many years from now, you will look back and not be able to remember exactly how everything worked out. But you will look back and see that God provided, your children did not starve, your home did not fall down from the rafters, your sleepless nights with newborn babies came to an end and you survived.

Let His rest see you through today, and be blessed in His presence.

Week Sixteen, Day 1

Where does your peace, or lack thereof, come from?

There is only one source of peace that lasts, which will sustain us through the longest days and the darkest nights. It is the peace that Jesus gives. The peace that trusting Him and resting upon His promises provides.

When we rest in Him, our hearts are fully and truly at rest. When we attempt to "rest" in anything else (television programs, chocolate bars, bubble baths, lattes, exercise, etc.) we find ourselves jumbled and still stressed.

There is no substitute for Jesus' blessed peace. He will continue to draw your heart toward His for as long as it takes you to realize the world offers no peace that can compare with His peace. He is patient.

Don't make Him wait, or waste any more days. Set your heart at rest in His presence and receive the peace that surpasses all understanding. His peace overcomes the world and its woes.

Enjoy His peace today and resolve to rest in it from here on out.

Week Sixteen, Day 2

"There is no ideal place for us to serve God except the place He sets us down." – Charles Haddon Spurgeon

Homeschooling can be overwhelming. Exhausting. Beyond anything we ever imagined it might be. It can also be rewarding. Gloriously enjoyable. A delight which we never expected.

If God has set you down in your home, with your children, and called you to homeschool, then you can count on the fact that He will be with you every single day. He will see you through. He will not fail you.

Don't waste your days dreaming of some more ideal life and ministry, because I believe Spurgeon had it right. Your ideal life and ministry is the place where God has set you down.

Embrace it, enjoy it, and at times just muddle through it. But do not forget that it is His ideal place for you.

Where He puts you is where He wants you. Don't try and run away to another, better place, similar to the Old Testament prophet Jonah. Rather, thank God for this place where He has placed you. Settle your heart on the matter and know that He knows best and that He is indeed very good to you.

Are you a Type-A perfectionist, work-a-holic mom? Perfectly penned lesson plans with perfect little check marks on each line upon completion? Bookshelves organized by subject, by author, and by book size?

Is your pantry tidier than a grocery store shelf? Cans stacked in perfect columns and rows, evenly spaced? Spices aligned by use, jar size, alphabetically?

Dinner menus planned a month in advance. And no "repeats", such as Meatloaf Monday, Taco Tuesday, etc.?

Color coordinated hair bows for each little girl's outfit. Cloth diapers perfectly folded on the middle shelf of the changing table. Photos on the mantle sitting at just the right angle.

If this is you, you may be wondering how on earth I know you so well, being that we have never met. Well, I am pretty Type-A myself. My solution has been to lower my unrealistic, ridiculous expectations.

This has been important for me as I have learned to live a more relaxed lifestyle. The Lord's will is for us to enjoy our homes and our families, and it is difficult to do that if the fingerprint on the window pane is more important than reading a storybook to our preschooler.

Lower your expectations in order to enjoy the family God has given you.

Week Sixteen, Day 4

If you're not exactly a Type-A mother, say you are a bit more spontaneous, go with the flow, who needs a plan anyway kind of homeschooler, my advice is simple. Raise the bar a little more for yourself.

Write out a week's worth of lesson plans on Sunday afternoon and then stick with the plan all week long. No rabbit trails allowed!

Plan menus for the entire week. If dinner menus seem too difficult to plan out, then start by planning lunches for the week. Or even breakfast. Then stick with the plan!

Just as lowering expectations is the key to a more relaxed homeschool life for the Type-A woman, raising the bar and adding structure is the key to a more relaxed life for a free-spirited homeschooler.

You don't need to give up all of your spontaneous ways. Just add a bit more organization to your day and then enjoy the benefits. Try it, you may really like it!

Week Sixteen, Day 5

<u>Habakkuk 3:18</u> – yet I will rejoice in the Lord, I will be joyful in God my Savior.

We have much to rejoice about; and we should be sure that we are a rejoicing people. Not a grumbling, cranky, discontented people.

Jesus' followers ought to be the most joyous people around! Yet often, we are just the opposite. Why is that? What cause do we really have for our sour attitudes and gloomy demeanors?

Life gets us down. The daily drudgery and trying heartaches. For homeschoolers, the never-ending challenges unique to our lifestyle can leave us feeling anything by joyful. And truly, that can be said of all who live in this fallen world, no matter their occupation.

Combating this is as simple, and as difficult, as rejoicing in the God of our salvation. Just begin to list the things He has done for you, and soon enough you will be thankfully filled with joy. The difficulty comes in choosing to reflect in His goodness daily. Make it a habit, and you will catch yourself smiling!

Week Seventeen, Day 1

It's easy for us homeschool moms to justify some extra time spent "improving our homeschool". We can search for creative ideas on Pinterest, soak in a bubble bath while reading our favorite homeschool magazine cover to cover, or run off to the library to gather some books for upcoming studies. None of these is wrong, but spending too much time "improving" can be detrimental to our marriages and our children.

More than a well-prepared mom, our kids need us to simply be fully there as a mom. Husbands don't need a perfectly organized closet as much as they need a wife who loves and respects them. And those who are watching us as we live out this homeschool lifestyle (in particular those who may be wondering if homeschooling is an option for their family) need to see us enjoying the life we're living rather than always striving to "improve" our life...which sometimes is more about "escaping" from our commitments than making improvements, if we are totally honest.

Be a choosey mom and be aware of how you spend your time. And if you really, truly want to know how you're doing as a wife and mom, then take a deep breath, be brave, and - GULP!! - ask your spouse and children. Once they know that you *really* want to know how they feel, they will tell you the flat out honest truth. If it's a truth that reveals areas in need of change, be brave enough to make those changes with the Lord's help.

This parenting thing is too important to put off until later. And your marriage is a life-long commitment that deserves your best day in and day out. Remember, you took wedding **VOWS**...not wedding Maybe-If-I-Feel-Like-Its.

You might just be surprised how much improvement will suddenly show up in your life by simply putting a damper on the amount of time you spend working to make improvements!

Week Seventeen, Day 2

Today, be radical in your obedience to the Lord and trust that your obedience matters.

Homeschooling is a fairly radical lifestyle. Taking on the responsibility for your children's education, and swimming against the tide of culture, is our daily life. Radical? Yes, we do radical pretty well.

Are we radical in our obedience to the Lord, in every area of our lives, however? In those areas that are most challenging? That bring no reward or recognition? Do we have feet that rush to do God's will? Are we radically obedient women?

Our obedience does matter. For us as individuals, for our families, and to the Lord. Be radical in your obedience today.

If you know me, then you probably know that I am none too fond of the self-help mentality. It's not that I have anything at all against people in need of help; I put myself at the top of the list of people who need help! But the notion that I can somehow fix myself ~ let alone fix anyone else ~ is a complete misnomer. It's a continual cycle of "work harder" followed by gut-wrenching disappointment. And there's a reason this is the cycle of self-help...it's because we *cannot* fix ourselves! That's God's job, and He's exceptionally good at it.

Having said that, I would like to mention something we moms DO have the ability to change for the better. Our attitudes. I will even go so far as to say that I feel many homeschool mothers could benefit from an attitude adjustment. We're often so tired, over-worked, and spread thin that we succumb to a bad attitude without any conscious effort on our part. It doesn't have to be this way! And I don't mean to say something contrary to my stance on self-help. I really think this one idea I'm about to share can have a positive impact on a mother'S attitude, and subsequently on the entire family.

So here is my novel idea. What if we went to bed each night having made the conscious decision to wake up thankful and happy the next morning?

The ramifications of a happy mother upon the family and the homeschool are incalculable. The happiness will spread and so will the thankful attitude. And a happy, thankful homeschool environment is really one of the greatest blessings a mom can receive.

Pray and ask the Lord to bless you with a happy demeanor and a heart full of thanks, and prepare to be amazed at how the Lord moves in your family.

Week Seventeen, Day 4

"God judges what we give by what we keep." – George Mueller

You don't have to have hoarding tendencies in order to hang on to things too tightly. Most of us living in westernized society do so to one degree or another. Yet God has a better way for us to live. He desires that we would hold tightly to Him and loosely to our possessions.

If you are a homeschool mother living on a limited budget, there can be a sense of need to hang on to curriculum and the like, just in case you need them at some point in the future.

This lends itself to self-reliance, which is essentially a lack of trust that the Lord will provide. It also involves the inability to be generous toward others. Both of these are detrimental to our walk with the Lord.

Look around your home, and think about those you know who have needs. Does anything you own seem more important than the people God has placed in your life? Even if you live in a state of great lack, you can still afford to pray for those who have needs. And most of us have ample enough supply to bake a dessert for someone, or drop a note in the mail to let someone know you are thinking of them.

Let what you keep be the measure of your generosity, rather than what you give.

Week Seventeen, Day 5

2 Corinthians 4:7 – But we have this treasure in jars of clay to show that this all-surpassing power is from God and not from us.

How often I become frustrated at my own shortcomings, character flaws and foibles. They annoy me as well as disappoint me. Yet these words from the Apostle Paul speak directly to my frustration. They tell me in no uncertain terms that I am a fragile, weak jar of clay. And that my fragility reveals that God's power, His all-surpassing power, comes from Him alone.

My flaws can actually draw people to Jesus, as unbelievable as that may sound.

But I do not like this truth. It almost aggravates me that I am so utterly unable to be of use in the Kingdom of God unless God Himself does the work in and through me. Did I not know this truth at the time of my salvation? Yes, of course I understood that he alone saved me; I could not save myself. How ridiculous of me to forget!

So I embrace myself as a fragile jar of clay, and I rejoice that he chooses to do His will in His strength alone. I learn, yet again, that all my hope is in Him alone. It is a good thing to be so fragile.

Week Eighteen, Day 1

What has been primarily occupying your thoughts as of late? What is on your mind and heavy upon your heart? Is it something worldly, something of the flesh, a particular fret or fear that is always there gnawing at you?

If this is the case, let me strongly encourage you to reset your mind on things above. Spend time praising God, for anything and everything, and do this every hour if need be until you are fixated on Him above all else.

Preoccupation with anything that is not God's best is truly a waste of time. And time is the commodity of greatest value for us, so it is not something we ought to waste.

A beautiful side benefit to this will be that your children will see you choosing to focus on the Lord above all else. We know more is caught than taught, so by all means let them catch a grateful heart from you!

Give Jesus your thoughts and you will find your days and eventually your years will be filled with His very best.

Week Eighteen, Day 2

Mark 7:8 – You have let go of the commands of God and are holding on to human traditions.

Homeschooling has swelled in size over the last few decades. What once was a rarity, a seeming anomaly, is now recognized as a legitimate form of education around the globe. And because of the intense struggle to legalize and even legitimize home education, it has in some ways become a tradition of man's own making.

We can become so focused on doing what God has called us to do that we forget the God Who called us. Then His work *in* us becomes our work *for* Him. Which in turn evolves into a man-made tradition. It bears a semblance of holiness, but it denies the power of God simply because the focus is askew.

Jesus said that apart from Him we could do nothing. And He is always truthful. Let's trust Him enough to keep our hearts set on Him alone and to lay aside any aspect of homeschooling that has become a tradition.

How can we know the difference? By asking Him to do His work through us as we abide in Him, and to honestly admit when we find ourselves focused more on the task than we are on Him.

Week Eighteen, Day 3

"We must never promise ourselves more than God has promised us." – Matthew Henry

How many times have I fallen into the trap of believing something was a promise from the Lord when in fact it was no such thing? More times than I can accurately recall. Far too many times and always to my detriment.

I certainly want to grow in my understanding of God's Word, to grow in my faith, to grow in my ability to appropriate His sure promises. I also need to grow in my ability to discern when a promise was created by me, in my own heart and mind, and then attributed to the Lord.

This can be difficult, but it is vital for my spiritual health. Constantly mishearing from the Lord (which is actually my own voice speaking far louder than His voice) leaves me discouraged and distraught, both of which are tools the enemy uses against me.

The only answer to this dilemma is to remain very close to Jesus, and when I do fall into the trap, I must reset my heart on Him immediately. I remind myself that the real treasure is not in the promise; the real treasure is the One who makes the promise.

Week Eighteen, Day 4

What's in my homeschool? What's in your homeschool? Is the joy of the Lord there? Is the Holy Spirit leading and guiding you throughout each day? Is there respect for your husband in your homeschool? Plenty of love and grace and mercy shown to your children? Is the Ancient of Days the ruler over all your minutes and your hours? Does the Great I AM have all authority over your homeschool – from curriculum choices to character building to sick days? Is all of your life and all of your homeschool laid upon His altar?

In the course of our day, may we remember that the very same God who told Moses that He would give him the ability to speak is the God who gives you words to speak to your children as you homeschool. Remember this is the very same God who gave Samson strength to slay a lion with his bare hands. Will He not also give us all that we need as we pour ourselves into our children day after day?

He truly does give us all we need for life and godliness, at all times. What a wonderful God we serve. May your home be filled with His aroma and may your homeschool bring much glory to His Name today.

Week Eighteen, Day 5

God makes us a spectacular promise when He says that all His promises prove true (see Psalm 18:30, Romans 3:4, and 2 Samuel 22:31). This promise encompasses all followers of Christ, and we can take it to the spiritual bank and cash this promise, with full confidence that there are more than sufficient funds.

God's assurance that each and every one of His promises will prove true is one of the most important spiritual truths that we can ever grasp.

Think of a verse that is dear to your heart, precious to you for one reason or another. Perhaps you have prayed this verse over your children for several years, or maybe you have laid claim to a specific portion of God's Word in regard to your marriage. How have you seen God answer those prayers? How has He acted on your behalf in response to your belief in His promises?

If you have not tried out God's commitment to keep His promises, be encouraged that He does have good things for you and He is wanting you to believe Him for those good things. When the road is rocky, could you try out some of His promises rather than give in to fret and worry? I am certain you will be pleasantly surprised by the wonderful results that come when trusting that all of God's promises to you will prove absolutely true.

And if you have trusted Him and seen that He is faithful to His Word, share that hope and encouragement with someone who needs to hear it. His good will toward His children knows no bounds, and His care for your concerns surpasses all understanding.

Be blessed by His promises today, and know He is always faithful and true.

Week Nineteen, Day 1

<u>1 Corinthians 8:1b</u> – But knowledge puffs up while love builds up.

Knowledge. What does that word bring to mind? As a long term homeschooler, knowledge has been my focus, my aim, and my agenda a lot of the time! I am often thinking of ways to grow in my own knowledge in order to better teach my children, and looking for ways to impart knowledge to them in order to prepare them for adulthood.

But here Paul says that knowledge puffs up. What image does that bring to mind? I think of a bird puffing out its chest in hopes of drawing attention to himself. Maybe the bird is attempting to secure a mate, or desires to appear mightier than he actually is as a means of self-defense.

Does my striving toward knowledge lead to either of these extremes in my life? Do I become arrogant? Am I attempting to draw attention to myself, and thus away from God? Do I use my knowledge to keep people at arm's length, in an attempt to protect myself from possible harm? After all, real relationships come with real risks. Am I avoiding risk via knowledge?

Let me rather choose love on a daily basis, and build others up even as God in His great love builds me up. Let me be known as a woman who loves.

Week Nineteen, Day 2

<u>Isaiah 30:19c,d</u> – at the voice of thy cry, when He shall hear it, He will answer thee... (King James Version)

What a wealth of comfort and assurance this verse from the book of Isaiah brings. We have here the full, the complete, the total, all-encompassing promise that as soon as we begin to give utterance to our prayers, our God hears and He promises to answer.

While we typically would like an immediate answer, and often a predetermined and specific one, this verse does not provide that promise. God is, after all, God Almighty, not a wish granting genie of the lamp.

The real comfort of Isaiah 30:15 is the assurance that He hears us, and that He hears instantly.

Do you hear your children the very moment they make a sound? Not always. However, God does hear us from the first moment we speak. What a comfort, what a loving Father.

How close would you need to be in order to hear your child from the first sound, the first syllable? That is exactly how close your God is to you when you speak to Him in prayer.

Take comfort. He will answer. Take greater comfort in this; He is very near and He does hear you.

Week Nineteen, Day 3

I'm sure you've heard the saying: "To the victor go the spoils."

While that is true in the worldly sense, it is also true in the spiritual sense, particularly with regard to prayer.

If you only pray last-minute, state of emergency prayers, you probably will not gain many spoils. Sure, you will have some answered prayers and be rescued from some sticky situations, but you probably won't have a lot of deep, meaningful answers to long-term prayers. Because if you never engage in long, hard battles but choose instead to burn your draft card and flee the fight, then you will never receive the spoils that often come only after the battle has been fought through and won.

Not just won – but first fought and then completely won.

Spiritual battles are real and they are vital if you want to be a mighty soldier in the Lord's Army.

Get in the mix, jump into the fray, engage in long-term prayers. The spoils are waiting for you. But you cannot have them if you are not in the fight.

Week Nineteen, Day 4

Isaiah 26:12 – Lord, you establish peace for us; all that we have accomplished you have done for us.

Are you in need of peace? Is your husband? What about your children? Does your homeschool need a good-sized dose of God's peace?

No matter what you do or don't do, it will never be enough to regulate your life so that it is peaceful. That is because the Lord alone desires to be our peace. Not our circumstances and certainly not our ability to control those circumstances! That's not true peace, anyway; it is just the façade that we can manage our lives apart from the Lord.

Do you have any accomplishment that you are proud of? Something that brings you great delight? This verse teaches that all we have accomplished has actually been accomplished by the Lord. He accomplished it for us.

Not only does He establish our peace, he also reminds us that we cannot accomplish anything without Him. Make Him Lord over all of your life, of your homeschool, and see how much He might accomplish through you.

Week Nineteen, Day 5

Do we, as homeschool mothers, ever try and hold on to our children too tightly? Is too much of our personal identity wrapped up in our children? If so, what will happen when they grow up and leave home?

My children aren't little anymore. Planning for graduations and filling out college applications and FAFSA forms has replaced sippy cups and diapers. Yes, my children are growing up…but am I?

More wrinkles? Check! Graying hair? Check! Allowing my children to grow toward adulthood without any guilt or manipulation on my part? Well…

I understand how difficult it is to pour all of yourself into this lifestyle known as homeschooling. It can be even more difficult to step back and let go as our children become young adults. But it's healthy and it's right to let go as God leads. Remember, we are training up the next generation. God has good plans for each of our children.

Seek His will for your life as you continue seeking His will for your children. He will help you to let go when you need to, and even in the letting go, He will never let go of you.

Week Twenty, Day 1

Acts 20:24 – However, I consider my life worth nothing to me; my only aim is to finish the race and complete the task the Lord Jesus has given me…

This is a simple, clear cut life goal. To fully grasp that our lives are worth nothing in and of themselves, that the only value of our lives is directly linked to Jesus and Jesus alone. This is tremendous and revolutionary. Getting this means a changed life, a new outlook.

Once we really grasp that our life is nothing without Jesus, it is easy to be content to simply finish the race and complete the task He has given us.

What is the task? What race are you meant to run?

It's not as hard to figure that out as you might think. What are you facing today? Homeschooling algebra? A husband out of work? A sick child? Potty training?

Complete the tasks that lie before you and ask God if you are missing anything. Run your race. It will become clearer, as you do today's work well with an attitude that remembers life without Jesus is nothing. Let Him refine your focus and continue to run your race all the days of your life.

Week Twenty, Day 2

Psalm 90:12 – Teach us to number our days, that we may gain a heart of wisdom.

While sitting outside during a garage sale, sort of scowling over the lack of sales, I began to consider whether I had been making the most of my time as of late. And if I hadn't been making the most of my time, then was I also failing to grow in wisdom? Was I expecting a behavior from my children that I wasn't requiring of myself? And what right did I have to be scowling about my unprofitable garage sale, anyway? That is certainly not worth frowning about.

While this particular summer had been very productive and enormously busy, I had to ask myself if that equated to making the most of my time according to God's desires. While much of my time had been well-used, there was a fair amount that had not been. Some of my time was probably squandered. No wonder I could not see much personal growth in wisdom. Thankfully the Lord used a silly garage sale to remind me of what was important.

I decided to go to the Lord and submit what remained of my summer to Him, asking the Holy Spirit to make the most of my time for His purposes, since I clearly was not doing so of my own accord. It was one of the best decisions I made that summer.

Ask the Lord to make the most of your time, and to bless you with a heart of wisdom.

Week Twenty, Day 3

An old saying says, "For the foolish, old age is like winter; for the wise, it is a harvest."

What truth does that speak to your mind and your heart as a homeschooling mother? What do you hear the Lord saying to you? How can you live today so that you will have a harvest in your old age?

Homeschooling has afforded me approximately three times as much time with my children as compared to sending them away to school. What have I done with all that time? Have I reveled in their hobbies and interests right alongside my children? Have I been there with them when they needed me most?

I have had so much time with my children as a result of our homeschool lifestyle. All the things I have enjoyed, the experiences I have had with my children, will be things I reflect upon in the winter years of my life. It is a unique blessing that only those who homeschool will truly understand.

Fully live in the times you are given, as you are given them. And don't dread old age; just embrace it as it comes.

Week Twenty, Day 4

John 5:30a – But I do nothing without consulting the Father. (New Living Translations)

The life of our Savior inspires me continually. One sentence written in red can do more to stir my heart than a hundred so-called inspirational books.

This verse from the fifth chapter of John urges me to follow hard after Jesus; may I do nothing without consulting the Father. How many grave errors do I make when I fail to consult with Him?

Perhaps it's just a habit, formed as a result of living in such a self-reliant society. We tend to pull up our boot straps and keep on keeping on. But we need to build a new habit into our lives wherein we seek God before we do anything at all.

This is a habit that will take a lifetime to perfect. Make it your heart's desire to fulfill God's will for your life. One way to accomplish that is to do nothing without first consulting your Father. Today seems like a good time to start.

Innocent. We often hear that word used to describe children. While it may seem correct in that children can be on the receiving end of evil with no ability to defend themselves, it is a completely inaccurate word, spiritually speaking.

Jesus said that there was no one good. Surely He did not forget children when He plainly used the words "no one". Other places in the Bible remind us that there is no one good, no not one. And that our hearts truly turn continually toward evil.

Just because we homeschool does not make this truth obsolete. Jesus' truth stands today, solid and unchanging as it ever has been. Our children have the same inclination toward sin that any other human being on this planet has. We are foolish to believe otherwise.

Continually point your children toward Jesus, the One who truly is good, and remind them to acknowledge their need of Him. Let homeschooling be a means to move them toward Jesus, not a means to believe that they are innocent and thereby have no need of a Savior.

Week Twenty-one, Day 1

Genesis 18:14a – Is anything too hard for the Lord?

What difficulties are you facing right now? A strong-willed child? Financial strain? An uncertain future for your husband at work? Aging parents? One particular subject that seems beyond your ability to teach?

How does the verse from Genesis 18 speak to your set of circumstances? Do you face each day's challenges with the calm assurance that no part of your day is too hard for the Lord to handle? Or do you allow anxiety, grumbling, fear and misery to govern your thoughts and control your attitude?

Try something new, if only for this one day. Believe this verse. Know that nothing you face is too difficult for your God. Ask Him to take control of these situations, to move mountains if need be, and to keep you from interfering in His plans for your family today. (Yes, we homeschooling mothers can interfere with God's will, believe it or not!)

Then tonight, as you lie down to sleep, be sure to thank Him for proving that indeed, there is nothing too hard for Him.

Tomorrow, start anew and remember the same promise will be true again.

Week Twenty-one, Day 2

When was the last time you felt frustrated?

For me, it was probably about ten minutes ago.

Frustrations are a part of life. Things don't go according to plan. People are inconsiderate and inconsistent. Circumstances are always in a state of flux. Homeschooling is just plain hard.

And so we can become frustrated.

But there is a solution for our frustration, and that solution is Jesus. When frustration comes, then it is time to run to Him. Pray and ask specifically that He fill you with His good and perfect and pleasing will for the situation. Which, I have found, always involves acting in love and kindness.

This isn't a pep talk. Nor is it a self-help segment that I saw on a morning talk show. You cannot do this on your own and neither can I. But if you ask, the Lord will do it through you because it will glorify Him.

So remember that frustration, when yielded to Jesus, becomes kindness. And that is a wonderful thing indeed.

"A man is what he thinks about all day long" – Ralph Waldo Emerson

How right Mr. Emerson was!

Do you want to be a grouchy woman? Then spend your day thinking about all the laundry you have to do, the dishes piled up in the sink, the finances, the math you still need to grade, the neighbor whose children are rude, and maybe spend a few minutes pondering how much you dislike working in the church nursery one Sunday a month. So, are you feeling grouchy yet?

Do you want to be a control freak? Think about your Pinterest boards, your meal plans, your lesson plans, your house cleaning schedule, your weight-loss program, your closet organizer. Let those thoughts fill your mind all throughout the day. Feel that control freak coming out?

Do you want to enjoy your children and husband more? Think about what makes them smile. Serve your husband's favorite meal for dinner. Be thankful for each of their individual personalities. Remember how much you love it when they really laugh that deep belly laugh.

Do you want to be a more godly woman? Spend your day thinking about God. Read His Word. Pray often. And you will become more godly day by day.

Week Twenty-one, Day 4

If I say the word "contagious", what comes to mind?

The flu? Ebola? A bad attitude?

Joy is also contagious. Infectious, even. And it is easy to start its spread.

Just decide that you will be constantly open to the joy that God offers. He will surely surprise you with more joy than you would have expected. He will fill you to overflowing. Your joy will be complete, because it will be found in Him.

Not only will it fill you, the joy of the Lord will be your strength. Which must surely mean that a joy-less mother is a strength-less mother. No homeschooling mother can afford to be strength-less. By all means, grab hold of that joy!

Make today a day of contagious joy. Spread it around to your family and friends. I promise, you will not regret it!

Week Twenty-one, Day 5

Psalms 90:17b – establish the work of our hands for us – yes, establish the work of our hands.

Homeschooling women spin a lot of plates, all day long, every single day. Some even homeschool on Saturdays in order to complete each year's curriculum. Many homeschool year round in order to meet all the needs of all their children, which can be seemingly impossible over the course of a traditional nine-month school year.

The work of a homeschooling mother's hands can be overwhelming. We need the Lord to establish our work, or we can expect to live our lives in a continually dumbfounded state.

So how, exactly, do we allow God to establish our plans?

First, spend time with the Lord daily. Read the Bible, pray, sit quietly before Him and listen. This is the most important part of your day. Be careful not to neglect it!

Second, be willing to not only hear what He says, but to do what He says. He will tell you what you need to know, but you must listen and obey.

Ask Him to establish the work of your hands today. Then do whatever He says to do. He alone knows how to keep us under-whelmed.

Week Twenty-two, Day 1

Psalm 34:19 – Many are the afflictions of the righteous, but the Lord delivers him out of them all.

We were never promised a life of ease anywhere in the Bible. In fact, we are warned against expecting that kind of a life through the many Bible verses regarding adversity. Homeschoolers are no exception to this reality.

Take courage from Psalm 34 when your times are full to the brim with trouble and there is no end in sight. The Lord has promised to deliver you out of all those troubles, and by "all", the Lord means every single one.

For the homeschool family, each school day provides an opportunity to trust the Lord through ever-changing troubles. Consider that in the course of a single day, you could be teaching one child how to read and a few minutes later be helping another child with their French lesson. Shortly thereafter comes a driving lesson for your teenager and then a biology lab. A homeschooling mother has a life that changes constantly. We meet the needs of many and often do so when it seems all strength is gone.

And when He keeps His promise and delivers us out of all afflictions? (Which, of course, He always does!) Do not forget His deliverance, or His love and grace that carried you through. Thank Him. Praise Him. Love Him. He is indeed a Mighty Deliverer.

Homeschooling mother, who is it, exactly, that gave you the life you now live? Was it man? Was it you? Or was it God?

Oh, it was indeed God. No man, no woman, could concoct such a life as the one you live, could they? It was most certainly God who ordered your life as it now is.

Pause for a moment and really recognize that as truth. You educate your children in your own home because God ordered your life this way. Are you thankful to Him for your life? Or have you taken for granted that this life is His gift to you?

Evaluate your attitude to discover whether or not you are truly thankful. There have been no enormous errors or mistakes that somehow landed you here. There is only God Almighty, the Sovereign One. He is trustworthy, and He loves you. And He does not make mistakes.

Your life is a gift. Be sure to remember that, and thank Him for it.

Judges 2:10 – After that generation had been gathered to their ancestors, another generation grew up who knew neither the Lord nor what he had done for Israel.

When we presumptuously assume that our love and commitment to the Lord will automatically be the standard for the next generation, we leave a door wide open through which the enemy of our souls can enter. Where the enemy finds an open door, you can be sure he comes directly in. What must we do in order to shut tight the door of presumption and assumption?

Much like the Israelite nation in the second chapter of Judges, we live in a society that seems to have forgotten God along with all He has done. The laws that govern our land and the behaviors which are no longer shocking are ample proof that the God of previous generations is not known very well in this modern age. The door was left open, and the enemy came right on in. There was no guard over the hearts of the people who now call evil good and good evil.

Our obligation to our children and to our God is to speak loudly of all that the Lord has done for us, and to proclaim Him to the next generation. Of course we cannot force our children to follow the Lord any more than you can force a horse to drink after leading him to water. However, you can run the horse pretty hard and feed him salt…you can make him thirsty and then see if he drinks the water. Pray that the Lord will give your children a thirst for Him and for His Word. Talk of all that He has done for you.

Take a stand, spiritually speaking, and guard the door to ensure it remains securely closed. Lead them to the Living Water as often as you can. This is how we fight for the next generation.

Week Twenty-two, Day 4

I found this written in an old journal of mine: "If men speak ill of you, live so that no one will believe them."

Although I do not know who first said those wise words, I do know that they speak loudly to my heart.

I have been spoken of in ways that were untrue. I am sure you have, as well. As a mother who has homeschooled for almost twenty years, believe me when I say I have heard my fair share of negative and derogatory comments about homeschoolers.

All of those things that people have said to you about homeschooling, those same things have been said to me. Often these hurtful words come out of the mouths of complete strangers! Of course, family and close friends have also questioned our decision to homeschool, and that was very difficult to hear.

Often I said very little in response to the questions. At the Lord's leading, many times I simply answered them in a non-confrontational manner while avoiding the more personal and prying aspects of their barrage. Believe me, this was the Lord's doing because I had plenty that I wanted to say!

And yet, in God's due time, I have had many of those same people share how they see things differently now. Tales of ways our children's lives have had profoundly impacted them and their family life. Remarks about wishing they had the diligence and tenacity to live the life that we have lived, so that they might see the results that we have seen.

I now know that a homeschool life well-lived can undo ill-spoken words. I pray you are able to keep living your family's homeschool life well, and that one day your accusers may all be quieted.

"The world expects, and rightly, that the Christian should be more gentle, and patient, and generous, than he who does not profess to be a disciple of the Lord Jesus." – Mark Guy Pearse

The truth pierces the heart like a saber, doesn't it? Truth cuts right through all the nonsense and brings our excuses into the cold, harsh light of day. The truth is powerful and can bring about needed change. This quote from Mark Guy Pearse is one such truth.

Mothers cannot be screaming at their children and acting out in a rage and still believe that the world sees Christ when it looks at them. Mothers cannot openly ignore their children when they are misbehaving, nor when they cry out with a need, and yet think the watching world sees them as examples of Christ and His great love. The world really does expect more from us. The problem may be that we expect so little from ourselves.

Are you *more* gentle, *more* patient, *more* generous than those who are not disciples? If not, don't you think you ought to be?

Not only is there a watching world, but your children are watching as well. They are living under your spiritual umbrella, so to speak. Are you certain that your umbrella is protecting them and shepherding them? Or has the umbrella blown away, leaving them exposed to the world and all its elements?

You are a disciple of the Lord Jesus. Today, behave as such.

Do you think of homeschooling as your full-time job? Or is it more like a part-time position? What I am asking is, are you fully engaged in your homeschool work, or just so-so?

This is not a question about whether or not you work outside of your home. Some of us have to work, it simply is not an option. What I am asking is, "Where's your heart?" You can be 100% dedicated to homeschooling and also work a full-time job. Or you can be a stay-at-home mom who homeschools and be 100% elsewhere with your attitude and your focus.

So I ask again, "Where's your heart?" Are you taking your God-given role as a mother seriously? Do you spend time praying over your homeschool and your children? Would your husband describe you as a fully engaged mother? How do you think your closest friends might describe you?

I am not trying to discourage you. In fact, my purpose in all my writing is to encourage homeschooling mothers and spur them on toward maturity in Christ. Asking ourselves the hardest questions can propel us on in the maturing process. Making sure we are fully engaged with our children as we homeschool only sets us up for success.

Let God put your heart where he wants it today.

Week Twenty-three, Day 2

<u>Psalm 34:17a</u> – The righteous cry, and the Lord heareth (King James Version)

Since we are made righteous in God's sight by Jesus' substitutionary death for us on the cross, we can cry out to the Lord and know with absolute certainty that He hears us.

This truth can be life-sustaining for a homeschooling mother. Often we barely have time to use the restroom in between laundry and meal preparation and co-op classes…and…and…and. Knowing that we can cry out to the Lord in the midst of our daily chaos, with the assurance that He hears, is of tremendous value. This understanding brings great comfort.

Of course, we have a real enemy with his own evil schemes and agenda. He does not want us to cry out to the Lord. Why is that? Because our enemy knows that God will hear! And if He hears, He also answers. So you will constantly be tempted *not* to cry out to the Lord.

Don't give up or give in, do not roll over and play dead. Keep crying out, keep trusting in the Lord, keep your eyes and your heart open for God's answers.

Do this in addition to your daily time spent in the Word and in prayer. This crying out type of prayer is not a substitute for your time with God each day; it is in addition to that precious time. Like any other relationship, you must foster growth. Staying close to the Father and crying out to Him often is an excellent way for such growth to occur.

Doing the same thing over and over again will not simplify your homeschool.

Griping to your husband each evening will not simplify your homeschool.

Changing churches, changing jobs, changing homes, changing friendships will not simplify your homeschool. Neither will cooking gourmet meals, grinding your own wheat, purchasing a new math curriculum, generating more income, subscribing to another newsletter, joining a local co-op, having your older children graduate, and even working in your own strength toward a more efficient daily schedule.

Nearly two decades of homeschooling has taught me these hard truths. It would be a blessing to me if other women did not have to learn them the hard way, through similar trial and error.

I have done a lot and seen a lot within the homeschool world. And I have found that tweaking the externals has never helped to simplify our homeschool.

But it's not all bad news! I am not saying there is no possible way to live a simpler life as a homeschooling family. There is a way; it is Jesus' way.

A central focus on Christ and a daily dependence upon the Holy Spirit is the only way to really simplify anything. This is no one-size-fits-all plan that I am pitching here. Jesus only works in personally customized solutions. He alone knows what is ideal for your children, for your family in your current season of life.

He delights to reveal His custom made plans to us, but we must draw near to Him and seek Him first. Put your relationship with Jesus first and He will begin to simplify your life.

<u>Galatians 6:7</u> – Do not be deceived: God cannot be mocked. A man reaps what he sows.

This verse contains a truth that eludes many people. So often we just keep on keeping on, living our lives helter-skelter, willy-nilly, never minding that what we sow we will also reap. How foolish we are!

Our daily choices make up the sum of our lives. There are no "free days" that fail to count toward eternity.

Our lives are to be hidden with God, in Christ. What we do with our days makes up the sum total of our lives. So our days must be aligned with Jesus' will - this is what it means to be hidden in God with Christ. Again, there are no "free days".

Sow bountifully and with quality seed today, my fellow homeschooling mother! Because a harvest is soon coming and only what is planted in Christ will last.

James 4:17 – If anyone, then, knows the good they ought to do and doesn't do it, it is sin for them.

What, specifically, is the good we ought to be doing?

This is a key question for the busy homeschool mother. Are we just supposed to roll out of bed in the morning and do whatever comes to mind? Or are we to be more intentional than that? If so, how intentional? Should we do all the planning for all the hours of all the days that we homeschool? And what, if anything, are we to be doing in addition to homeschooling?

I think the answer is both simple as well as complex.

The only way to really know the good that you ought to be doing is to rely on the Holy Spirit. He can, and He will, lead you into the light of God's will for your life, and that includes your homeschool. So the answer is simple; ask the Holy Spirit. But the answer is also complex; ask Him daily, perhaps even hourly, and do not freeze out of fear when the thing He calls you to do seems scary and outside your comfort zone.

Remember that whatever He calls you to do, He will actually be doing through you. We are truly never alone when we do God's will, and it should be much more frightening for us to be outside of His will than in it.

Week Twenty-four, Day 1

2 Corinthians 10:18 – For it is not the one who commends himself who is approved, but the one whom the Lord commends.

Seeking to find approval regarding our decision to homeschool is a sticky trap many of us have fallen into. It can be difficult to feel as if you are on the outside looking in. It is hard to see our children feeling the same way. As tough as it is to feel left out, we must remember that we have been commissioned by the Lord to homeschool. Our acceptance and approval must come from Him alone, even if that means we sometimes feel left out.

Besides, the accolades of the world always ring hollow. Doing the Lord's will as we trust in Him to defend us before all our critics leads to a life of abundant blessing. None of His loving words to us will ever ring hollow. And that is a lesson worth learning, for us and for our children.

Be encouraged that you are in excellent company if you are lacking in the area of support. Think of the greatest men and women in the Bible who often faced life with God alone as their source of strength and support; He will support you, too.

When you homeschool multiple children, it can be difficult to find ways to spend quality time with each child one-on-one.

There are many great ideas that I have seen through the years about how to divide your time among your children. Yet one that I feel serves the homeschool lifestyle best is to schedule Bible reading time together.

Choose a version that suits your child's age and reading ability. Have her read to you, and then you take a turn and read to her, and so on. Whether it's a picture Bible for toddlers or the King James Version for your teens, this is an excellent way to spend time, one-on-one, with each one of your children.

Count the time spent reading as your Bible curriculum for the day. Enjoy chatting leisurely, not academically, with them after you have finished reading. And be amazed at how much you will learn by studying the Bible alongside your children.

Week Twenty-four, Day 3

"Walking by faith means being prepared to trust where we are not permitted to see." – Jonathan Blanchard

I cannot think of a lifestyle that allows a mother to be fully reliant upon God day in and day out more than homeschooling does. We cannot do it all on our own, and we know that we can't! It is a walk of faith unlike any other in our modern society. Jonathan Blanchard's words are true for us in ways that he never could have imagined. I think he sums up our daily dilemma perfectly; we must trust where we are not permitted to see.

So where is it that you are not permitted to see right now? We all have at least one area of our lives that seems to be shrouded in mystery, where the future is uncertain. Our husbands do, as well. And of course, so do our children. Be aware that every member of your family is facing the unknown in one way or another. Remind them of the truth found in Blanchard's wise words.

Are you prepared to trust where God has not permitted you to see? Trusting God is always worth the risk.

Week Twenty-four, Day 4

False promises.

They are everywhere in our ad-saturated society. Sadly, plenty of homeschoolers participate in false advertising too.

Whether promising brilliant children, protection from all known sin and temptation, perfectly happy families, or even siblings that never ever argue – we, as a whole, are often selling a lie.

It really isn't fair to try and make people want something that we don't exactly have. And it's certainly not fair to our children when we expect them to portray a falsehood!

We are people living alongside other people. We all sin, we all make mistakes. The watching world does not need any more phony advertising and false promises. What they do need are real families who really love Jesus and are being real on a daily basis.

Let homeschooling be a source of God's grace and freedom for your family. Lay aside unrealistic expectations and false fronts. Let Jesus draw others to Himself through your very real family.

Week Twenty-four, Day 5

      1 Chronicles 5:20b – they cried out to him during the battle. He answered their prayers, because they trusted in him.

      You don't ever have to battle it out on your own. You may not even need to prepare for the battle! Just cry out to God and trust in Him to help you, the same way the Israelites did in 1 Chronicles chapter 5.

      He truly is trustworthy. He really will aid you as you seek to home educate your children for His glory. But you'll never know that for yourself if you do not cry out to Him when you see a battle headed your way.

      My homeschool battles have often been about math. And I'll tell you, I cannot win on my own. I lose my cool and blow it as a mom. The only hope I have is to cry out to my God, and keep crying out if my child continues the battle. He answers, He shows up strong, and my trust in Him grows and grows.

      Cry out to Him. Trust in Him! Find your hope, your peace, and your rest in Him.

Week Twenty-five, Day 1

Proverbs 16:31 – Gray hair is a crown of glory; it is gained by living a godly life. (New Living Translation)

I discovered my first gray hair when I was in my twenties. I was completely taken aback! How on earth could the process of aging be progressing so rapidly? Wasn't I too young for gray hair?

Then I regained my focus, reset my heart's attitude, and remembered that vanity is a stumbling block to a close walk with the Lord. For me, a focus on something like gray hair is truly, simply, a sin. As is anything that draws my heart and my desire away from Him.

Gray hair happens. And according to the book of Proverbs, it is a crown of glory that is gained by living a godly life. Isn't it wonderful that our loving God provides such comfort about something that is so inconsequential in light of eternity?

So don't fret about going gray. Rather, choose to thank your loving Father that He has marked you with a crown.

Week Twenty-five, Day 2

Proverbs 17:22 – A cheerful heart is good medicine, but a crushed spirit dries up the bones.

Often the beginning of a new homeschool year is filled with excitement and expectation. But the middle of the year, primarily that long stretch from January to March, can bring feelings of gloom and weariness. It is during this season that I do not come by a cheerful heart very easily. It sometimes feels as if I do not have the strength to homeschool thoroughly. I am exhausted and feel just plain sapped.

While I cannot manufacture a cheerful heart, I can opt to seek out beautiful aspects of the dreary winter months. Sometimes a simple thing provides me with a cheery heart; a toasty fire, a hot cup of tea, a worn out favorite book. The one thing that can always bring a smile to my heart is the hum of my Kitchen Aid mixer when I am baking. It may sound odd, but all my stress melts away when I am mixing batter for Pumpkin Chocolate Chip Bread or adding my secret ingredient to a batch of banana bread.

When my strength is renewed, I can get through even the longest dreary, winter day with a thankful heart and a much improved disposition. Praise the Lord for the little ways He blesses us with joy. Praise Him for His Word that daily loads me with benefits.

Week Twenty-five, Day 3

Wouldn't it be terrific if there were a lovely package delivered to your front door a few times each school year, meant just to encourage you on your annual homeschool journey?

Just think of it; your favorite tea or coffee, a brand new mug or tea cup, maybe a pretty new journal and several pens and the like. Something special, just for you, the homeschool mom.

I'm not one to advocate loads of selfish "me time", but I am one to advocate homeschooling mothers taking the time to make each academic year a positive experience for themselves as well as for their children.

Maybe I can't send each and every homeschooling mother a beautiful gift box filled with her favorite things. But I can encourage each of us to allow the Lord enough access into our hearts and lives to keep us joyful. For Him to fill us up to overflowing. To know He has good plans for our future.

Remember today how great is the Father's love toward you. Take heed from one of the most vital, life-giving lessons that the Lord has taught me: *You Are Allowed to Enjoy Your Life.*

So allow yourself to enjoy your life today. God wants you to!

"Do not go about your service of God as slaves to their taskmaster's toil, but run in the way of His commands because it is your Father's way." – Charles Haddon Spurgeon

If your role today is to teach grammar and times tables, then run in it rather than toil at it. Whether it's laundry or illness or even great celebration, it is all doable in the strength that results from the joy of the Lord.

When we embrace our Father's way as good and even very good, His beautiful gift to us, then the way we live our lives is truly changed. Serving God becomes a treasure instead of a burden. His commands feel light and are even enjoyable. No good thing does He withhold from those who walk uprightly.

He isn't a harsh taskmaster. Don't think of Him as such. Believe He is a loving God, and He will not disappoint you.

Romans 8:6b – but the mind governed by the Spirit is life and peace.

A mind controlled by the world, by the flesh, by the enemy of God is a mind filled with chaos and unease. As my daughter would say, that mind is like "a bag full of cats"!

The mark of the Spirit's control of your mind is life and peace. Having God's peace means having a sense of inner calm, regardless of circumstances, coupled with the ability to hear from the Lord and think clearly. It is the opposite of a panicked mind filled with jumbled thoughts. We can pray to have a peaceful mind, knowing that this is God's will for us.

There is also the promise of life when the Holy Spirit controls one's mind. Life is the opposite of death. Deadly thoughts are doubtful, discouraging, angry, hate-filled, believing the worst about people and situations. If this describes your thought life, get away and pray, asking the Spirit to renew your mind according to His will. Seek Him for His peace and His life.

This is yours for the asking, it is a promise given to you. You have been blessed with the mind of Christ. Do not allow your enemy to tell you otherwise.

Week Twenty-six, Day 1

Psalms 121:3b –he who watches over you will not slumber.

Do you ever wonder if God has forgotten you? Or perhaps, does it seem He has forgotten some specific problem you need Him to take care of?

It sounds trite and you have heard it before, but it is worth repeating. He who watches over you does not sleep or slumber. And He is capable of keeping safe all that you have entrusted to Him.

Take all of your problems and place them at His feet with an attitude of thankfulness. Fully entrust your concerns to Him – homeschool related or not – and *act as if* you believe that He who watches over you will not slumber. Thankfully watch for Him to answer on your behalf. In His time you will see Him move.

He who keeps you will not slumber, not even for a moment. The God of the universe will never be caught napping on the job. You are un-forgotten, un-forsaken, and you can truly be un-shakable in Christ Jesus.

Week Twenty-six, Day 2

There really is a plan, and the Master Planner is trustworthy and good.

We all know Jeremiah 29:11, and we say that we believe it. Yet if we look at the way we live our lives day by day, from the perspective of an outsider looking in, would we still be able to say we actually live out Jeremiah's words?

Try this, just for today. Remind yourself over and over again that your loving Father has plans for you, that those plans are good and filled with hope. Safe, trustworthy, true plans.

Then live like you know that it is true. Because it absolutely is the truth! As true as the rising of sun and the daily ocean tides.

Finally, just for today, walk in sure confidence knowing that God's good and hope-filled plans for you cannot be thwarted or derailed.

Try this as an exercise in faith. And hopefully, after doing it for just one day you will do it again tomorrow, and then again the day after that. Until it becomes a way of life that outsiders looking in will use to describe you and your God.

Week Twenty-six, Day 3

<u>Psalm 103:2</u> – Praise the Lord, I tell myself, and never forget the good things he does for me. (New Living Translation)

Sixteen words…and if I could just do as they say, how different my day-to-day life would be!

I love that Psalm 103 says, "I tell myself" in the New Living Translation. Oh yes, the author of this psalm really gets it! This is how we homeschooling mothers operate, is it not? We have to tell ourselves what we most need to remember. Don't we do it all the time?

I repeatedly tell myself things such as: "Don't forget to find the missing Biology answer key…find that answer key…remember to go downstairs and look for that lost Biology key…" or "Get milk on the way home from piano lessons….don't forget you need milk…stop after piano and buy milk…" and "Remember to pay the electric bill tomorrow…don't forget about the electric bill…pay for the electricity tomorrow…don't forget…"

And then there is this one: "Praise the Lord…praise the Lord…praise You, Lord…let me not forget all the good things You have done for me…praise the Lord…"

The automatic result of continually reminding myself to praise the Lord is that I will not forget His benefits, so very much good which He has done for me.

Now, what is it that you need to remember to do today? Praise the Lord, that's what!

Who is it that encourages and inspires you? Think about that for a moment. It could be someone you know well or a person whose life you've only read about in books.

Whoever it is, there must be a reason, or several reasons, why they have brought inspiration and encouragement to your life. Can you pinpoint a couple of those reasons? Be specific.

Do those reasons have any Biblical correlations which you can make? A parallel you can draw between those specific traits and the Word of God?

An example could be someone who has a prayer life similar to Daniel's when faced with definite dire consequences, or some particular fruit of the Spirit that you long to exhibit.

Now consider how you might pay that trait forward to your children and your husband, friends and neighbors. Even to your enemies who do not much care for you.

We are inspired and encouraged not solely for our own well-being, but also so that we can share that encouragement with others.

Jesus was not stingy when sharing His great love. Let us not be stingy, either.

Guard what goes in and your heart will be far better off.

Homeschooling mothers, as a whole, are really good at guarding what our children see and hear. The books they read, who they spend time with, the movies they watch, all this and more is carefully considered and managed. But do we manage our own hearts with the same caution and tenacity?

There is just too much garbage that is too readily available at too many moments throughout the day. At any second we can see what is going in the world with a quick Google search. Often what we see is not something we would allow our children to look at.

Not every choice is a wisely made choice. Glancing at your smart phone while your son completes his spelling list is, quite frankly, and unwise choice. I do not need to explain why it is unwise; you already know. Truth is truth. It does not shock you to read these words.

The hard truth is that constant access to time-wasters and pop culture is of absolutely no eternal benefit. It damages relationships and poisons the heart.

Apply the same standards across the board in your home and watch God bless your wise choices.

Week Twenty-seven, Day 1

<u>Romans 1:11-12</u> – I long to see you so that I may impart to you some spiritual gift to make you strong – that is, that you and I may be mutually encouraged by each other's faith.

In Romans 1, verses eleven and twelve, Paul speaks of his desire to share a spiritual blessing with the church in Rome. His goal is to grow the believers up strong in the Lord. Do you desire that your children be strong in the Lord? Is one of your goals as a homeschooler to impart spiritual blessings and maturity to your children?

Specifically mentioned in verse twelve is the Apostle Paul's hope that the church in Rome would be able to encourage him in return. He did not view discipleship as a one-way street, with the teacher doing all of the admonishing and everyone else doing all of the growing. Rather Paul deeply wanted to see growth in his own heart and life, and he wanted it to come via mutual encouragement and edification.

If we never gather together with other members of the church, then this desire of Paul's can never be a reality in our lives. Mutual encouragement must happen in group settings. Social media will not accomplish this. We must meet with other Christians; it must be our priority.

Do nor forsake the gathering together of the saints, and don't assume that you have nothing to offer your fellow believers. Who knows that what you have to share, whether a kind word or a listening ear or a hard to share Biblical truth, might be just the catalyst someone needs to move forward with Jesus? Give and receive and grow together, united as a church, which is something our Lord prayed for us.

Joshua 5:7a – So he raised up their sons in their place…

In Joshua 5, verse seven we read that the children had grown up to take the place of their fathers. You remember that Joshua became the leader of the Israelites as they entered the Promised Land following the death of Moses. The book of Joshua details their conquests in this much hoped for land.

In this verse, if we use Strong's Exhaustive Concordance to better understand the word "up", we find that it means "to arise, become powerful; come on the scene, to be established, be confirmed; to be valid; to be proven; to be set, be fixed; to raise up, constitute". (KJV, Hebrew Strong's #6965)

So the two-word phrase "raised up" carries quite a lot of weight. Someday our children will each be raised up, established, validated and fully ready to leave our homes and walk into the Promised Land which the Lord has for them.

If we could fully grasp the fact that we are working primarily to equip our children for the next phase of their lives, and that our time with them is limited, how our homes and our homeschools would change! If we equip and prepare our children for every aspect of life yet leave them unprepared to live a life of God's choosing, we will have failed them.

We need to choose to work at the most important tasks first and foremost, and trust that all these other things will be added to them as well. Give them good, solid Biblical teaching each day and raise them up ready to come on the scene as men and women of the Lord.

How do you handle conflict with other homeschoolers?

Ah, now this is a difficult question! Many homeschooling mothers simply try to avoid conflict at all costs. Confrontation with our in-laws, our neighbors, the spiteful woman who sits behind you at church…some of us can handle those conflicts very well and they may not even take us by surprise. But conflict with our fellow homeschoolers? That is often another story altogether.

We have an unwritten rule, this expectation that our dealings with homeschool families will always be smooth sailing. And when conflict does arise we can be clueless as to how to handle it.

Remember, every homeschooler is just another human being with flaws and insecurities that are no different than your own. Each family has its own quirks and idiosyncrasies, the same as your family. People are often wounded, struggling and unsure of themselves. So of course there will be times of conflict.

Handle it the Lord's way – with grace, with love, and with prayer. At times He will lead you to remove yourself and your family from certain relationships. But He is a God of healing and restoration, so He will often call you to walk that path. He delights in us when we cooperate with Him in that process. Let Him lead and let Him heal.

Week Twenty-seven, Day 4

"Consider what you would have been but for divine grace." – Charles Haddon Spurgeon

Every now and then, dear homeschooling mother, stop and remember what your life was like before Jesus rescued you from sin and death. Consider just what your life might be like without Him.

Remind your children of the precious gift that Jesus' free, abundant grace truly is. Remind yourself, too! We live differently when we call back to mind what life would be like if only...

Having an attitude of gratitude is in keeping with a heart that loves the Lord. I have read many biographies of Christian men and women who greatly impacted the world for God's kingdom and have often seen a common thread that ran through each of their lives. At some point in time, they had an encounter with the Lord that clearly revealed to them their great need of a Savior and they were so overcome by His sacrifice and His love, they never were the same form that day forth.

Take stock of what you would have been, and let Him change you and then use you mightily for His glory and the furtherance of His kingdom.

"Consider quietly how impossible it is for God to lie." – Andrew Murray

I have never met a Christian who would outright call God a liar. However, I have met many Christians who live with such constant doubt that by their life, they imply that God does indeed lie.

Is this not one of the saddest experiences of immature Christians? Worse yet, it is tolerated and even excused! But how inexcusable it actually is to treat our Sovereign God as if He would ever lie. We confuse God's patience and grace for tolerance when we leave room for so much doubt in our lives. Our job is to propel one another toward growth and maturity, and we cannot do that if we don't address this problem of chronic doubt.

Andrew Murray's words tell us to consider with quietness how impossible, absurd even, it is to think that God would ever lie to us. His advice is to sit quietly with a listening heart in the Lord's presence while pondering why we would ever think Him capable of falsehood will reveal clearly how foolish that notion is.

Practice this quietness any time you find yourself doubting the Lord. It should quickly cure your wrong thinking.

Week Twenty-eight, Day 1

      <u>Psalm 10:13</u> – As a Father has compassion on his children, so the Lord has compassion on those who fear him.

      What a wonderful verse to teach us about good parenting! Our perfect Father in heaven is compassionate, slow to anger, and abounding in love. We will of course never be as loving and patient and compassionate as Almighty God, but by trusting Him to work in and through us, we can become compassionate parents.

      There are plenty of parenting books available at your local bookstore, with page after page of good advice. I do not discourage anyone from working to become a better parent. Reading these types of books can provide some insight and understanding, nuggets of wisdom that can be a blessing. God can use parenting books to grow us into better parents.

      I strongly encourage my fellow homeschooling mothers to filter everything that they read in those books through the lens of God's Word. Only then will we be able to know what the Lord's good and perfect and pleasing will is for us as we parent our children. His Book is the one we must read first and foremost.

Week Twenty-eight, Day 2

Have you found yourself feeling a bit worn out? Worn down? Just plain worn?

That is completely normal for a homeschooling mother. I would be very worried if you told me that you don't ever feel worn. In fact, I would probably tell you I thought you were lying to me. I doubt that any woman can homeschool for very long with facing some degree of worn-out weariness.

When you are worn, what do you do? Keep pushing, albeit at a much slower pace? Or do you find a way to relax and simply check out for a while? As tub full of Calgon? An hour of Candy Crush?

Try running to the Father the next time you feel worn. He is not a quick fix. He will not haphazardly patch up what is broken and send you back to work still feeling worn. No, He will rebuild. Renew. Restore. Re-invent.

God is too big to just provide an easy out or a feel-good fix. He is making you holy.

When you are worn, take it as an opportunity to be made new. As often as you need to be.

1 John 2:27 – But you have received the Holy Spirit, and he lives within you, so you don't need anyone to teach you what is true. For the Spirit teaches you all things, and what he teaches is true – it is not a lie. So continue in what he has taught you, and continue in Christ. (New Living Translation)

As a follower of Christ, you have the best life guide available to you – the Holy Spirit.

When you are struggling with teaching a new subject, or rather struggling to learn a new subject so that you will be able to teach it, ask the Counselor for help.

If you are feeling like an odd duck because so many women around you aren't homeschoolers, and when you see your children hurting because they also feel like odd ducks, let the Holy Spirit comfort you.

Maybe your children are unsure what they ought to do with their lives after high school. Let Him lead you, and lead each of them, along the best pathway for life.

There is never a time when you need to go about your life alone, and you do not have to bravely stare down your confusion and difficulties. The Holy Spirit is always there to help you. Talk to Him at any time about anything, and be sure to listen to His loving guidance.

Week Twenty-eight, Day 4

Our personal life often carries over to our children. I don't mean the times when we snap at them or lose patience with them due to extenuating circumstances in our lives.

I am referring to the fact that our children can absorb and take on our stress, even when we do our absolute best to keep that stress hidden from them.

There isn't very much we can do "in the flesh" about this problem, and quite honestly, some children are just prone to picking up on other's stresses. But spiritually speaking, we can cover our children in prayer and ask the Father to: **a)** eliminate any adult-stress that they should not be carrying and **b)** work in their hearts to equip them to not absorb and react to other people's stress.

In addition to covering them in prayer, we also need to give our children time and opportunities to talk openly about what concerns them. This should be done in a relaxed setting – probably not right before a science test, for example. After talking with them, be sure to comfort them and remind them that God's Word admonishes all of us to cast our anxiety upon Him because He cares for us. Confess any known worry that you may have displayed and pray with your child.

Trust the Lord to make your child less stress oriented.

Proverbs 29:1 – Whoever stubbornly refuses to accept criticism will suddenly be destroyed beyond recovery.

These words penned long ago by wise King Solomon aptly fit our lives today. I am so very grateful that I have grown in my ability to allow God's Word to teach and discipline me, which is often what I need and exactly what this verse delivers.

Here we are told that if we refuse to accept criticism, we will be broken beyond repair and it will happen suddenly, probably unexpectedly. That is a truly staggering thought. The honest truth is that I have been broken in areas of my life where I refused any correction or criticism. Thankfully, the Lord has worked in my heart, making me more accepting of criticism and critique.

No one really likes to be criticized, but the truth is we are all going to give and receive plenty of it, so we ought to learn how to deal with it. When we learn how to accept it with humility, we will in turn be better able to give criticism with love.

I would like to share a prayer for homeschooling mothers, asking the Lord to help us deal with the pain and pride of criticism.

Father, as homeschooling parents, we are often subject to criticism, from inside and outside the church. We need Your help to deal with it in a manner that glorifies You. Teach us to see all criticism through Your eyes, and to share criticism with Your words only. Show us how to love others so deeply that any criticism we might give would only be given for their benefit. Enable us to receive criticism in such a way that it would cause us to mature. Help us to bring any hurts we receive to You, so that You might comfort us and keep us from taking offense. Let no bitterness take root in our lives. We praise You for continuing to work in each of our hearts and homes. In Your Name we pray, AMEN.

We are all really just stewards. Of our money, our possessions, our time, our children. Are we being wise in the way we homeschool them? Can we say with confidence that we are examples of godly stewardship?

Keeping too long or too short a leash on our homeschool days is not good stewardship, any more than going into debt for worldly pleasures would be. Time is our friend if we use it as the precious resource that it is. It becomes our enemy when we misuse and waste it. And in the end, the enemy of our souls will remind us of all that we missed due to squandered time.

One thing I have found that greatly improves my stewardship is praying for each of my five children. For their learning struggles, which curriculum each child needs, extracurricular activities, friendships and relationships with siblings. I have a small notebook in which I write down what I sense the Lord is speaking to me regarding each child.

I do this in depth each summer, and then in shorter prayer sessions throughout the school year. It keeps me focused on the Lord as I homeschool and also is a frame of reference to see how far each child has come.

Stewardship is serious business. Make God-honoring stewardship a priority and know that as you seek His will for each of your children, He will indeed provide clear guidance.

Week Twenty-nine, Day 2

2 Peter 1:3-4a –By his divine power, God has given us everything we need for living a godly life. We have received all of this by coming to know him, the one who called us to himself by means of his marvelous glory and excellence. And because of his glory and excellence, he has given us his great and precious promises.

Oh how thankful I am that I don't have to figure out how to live a godly life all on my own. I would be a miserable failure at it, without even the smallest bit of success.

When I break down these verses from 2 Peter, I am reminded of how the process of godly living actually works in real life, flesh and blood. First I see that it is God's divine power that is the source of this life. Not any power of my own, not any power from my husband or my pastor. God's divine power. God the Father, God the Son, God the Holy Spirit are divine; this is their power. I am not its owner, I am just a recipient.

Next I find that God promises here to give me all that I need for living a godly life. I don't have to figure it out on my own. I do have to stay in communication with the One who gives all that I need.

But how do I get all this? By coming to know Him, and by staying close to Him. Through daily fellowship with Him.

It is His marvelous glory and excellence that accomplishes a godly life in me and in you. Aren't you glad it isn't something you have to manage in on your own? I know I certainly am.

Make it a priority to always ask what God's will is for any given situation or circumstance. Once He has revealed His will to you, be sure to obey Him and do anything He has asked of you. This is the path to an abundant life.

No matter what subject you may be preparing to teach in your homeschool, from kindergarten to 12th grade, seeking God's perspective should be a huge part of the process.

He knows your children best, and He has a plan for their education. Your job is to seek Him and hear what His plan is. He may not tell you all of the exact details, or which specific textbooks to purchase, but He will lead you and guide you day by day as you continue to homeschool for His glory.

Remember that it is a relationship you have with your loving Father, and were He simply to drop the answers to your every question in your lap, you wouldn't pursue Him in a relational way. Needing to remain in Him on a daily basis really is the best answer to every prayer. He is indeed a loving and wise God.

Week Twenty-nine, Day 4

Job 16:22 – Only a few years will pass before I take the path of no return.

Life is short. The older I get, the more I see how true this is. When I was very young, it seemed as if old age were far, far in the distance. Now it is right around the corner.

And when my children were little, it seemed as though they would remain little for a very long time. Now they are all adults or nearly so, and I wonder at where the time has gone.

Job 16:22 has it right; in just a few years we shall take the path of no return. There is no such thing as reincarnation within the belief system of the Christian. Like it or not, we only get to live out life on this planet once. Then we will step into eternity.

Be certain of your eternal future by accepting Jesus as your own personal Lord and Savior. Don't neglect to take care of the one matter that impacts all eternity. Share with others the love and message of Christ and the cross, and pray for many to come to knowledge of His truth.

Be a homeschooling mother who cares for others even while you care for your own family. Because the Lord wants all of us to be called children of God through faith in His Son Jesus Christ.

Romans 15:14 – I myself am convinced…that you yourselves are full of goodness, filled with knowledge, and competent to instruct one another.

Never doubt whether or not you are competent enough to homeschool your children. This verse from Romans declares that God says you are. And God's Word is true.

Romans 15:14 makes for an excellent memory verse that homeschoolers should recall as often as they need to. If you feel that you need some reassurance, then let this verse provide it. Let's look at what it says.

First, be convinced, certain, unwavering in your ability to teach your children. You should know that you know that you know that you can homeschool them. Second, remember that God says you are full of goodness. Of course, there is no woman who is good in her own nature, but because Christ indwells us, we are filled with His goodness. This is the truth; you may as well choose to believe it. Next it says that you are filled with knowledge. This is what you need in order to homeschool, isn't it? Well, praise the Lord, he has given you what you need!

And last of all is the beautiful assurance that you are competent to instruct one another. There is no disclaimer found here, stating that only those who were instructed by a particular apostle can instruct others, or only those who meet some other qualification. The only qualifier is being a disciple of Christ. If you are a disciple, then you are fit to instruct.

Be assured that you have all you need to homeschool your children. He promises that you do.

Week Thirty, Day 1

<u>Matthew 6:22</u> – The eye is the lamp of the body. If your eyes are healthy, your whole body will be full of light.

This is a verse I often pray over my college-age children. Specifically, that they would look upon those things that will move them toward holiness and look away from things that will not. What we look at, focus on, and visually engage with is what makes our "eyes" healthy or unhealthy. They are the lamp of the body. Not only do they allow "bad stuff" in when we focus on it, but they also project "bad stuff" out. As a lamp reflects its light outward, so our eyes reflect what is inside of us.

Keeping your focus on the Lord gives you healthy eyes – and subsequently, healthy eyesight. If this is true for you, it is also true for your children. Begin praying that your children's eyes would stay pure while they are young. Continue to pray for that when they are older. My adult children need my prayers as much now as when they were little. And who will pray for your children in the same manner which you do? Most likely, no one will. This is on you, mom!

Let your whole body be full of light – and seek God's favor that the same will be true of your children.

Is it possible that you homeschool out of fear?

Perhaps you have never considered this possibility before. Or maybe you know full well that fear governs your decision to homeschool.

God does not ever want His children to make decisions based on fear. Fear is a tactic of the enemy, and the only fear God employs is the fear of the Lord, which is a reverential awe of His greatness and an acknowledgement of His holiness.

Here are a few questions to ask yourself:

~ Are you hesitant to tell people that you homeschool?

~ Do you avoid social situations for yourself and your children?

~ Do you find yourself micro-managing even the smallest of details?

~ Are you ever nervous about answering the door or the telephone?

~Does the thought of college worry you more than it ought to?

~Is the weight of the world resting squarely upon your shoulders?

Answer these questions honestly and openly before the Lord. If you discover that you homeschool due to fear, renounce that fear in the Name of Jesus and accept the freedom that He offers. Homeschooling should be a work we partner with the Lord to accomplish, and in that partnership there is no room for fear.

Week Thirty, Day 3

Have you ever considered King David's wife Michal? I mean, really stopped and wondered at her life?

I have, and in doing so I realized a few things. I discovered that somewhere along the way, Michal, wife of King David, let herself become a bitter woman. Sure, her life had more than its fair share of trial and tribulation, and plenty of room for some angst and probably moments of fear. But becoming a bitter woman is a decision she made irrespective of her life's circumstances.

I imagine that a part of Michal's sour attitude was a direct result of her emotional separation from her husband. She did not care about the things he cared about; did not participate in his life's work. Perhaps she even considered herself to be King Saul's daughter rather than King David's wife.

As a homeschooling mother, I can easily wrap my entire identity in that job description. *Homeschooling Mother* could be the only way I think of myself. I can completly forget that I am someone's wife.

Through almost twenty years of home education, I have seen the damage that occurs when I forget my identity, and when I allow bitterness to creep into my heart. As I sit before the Lord daily, I ask Him to remind me who I am and to tear out any root of bitterness.

As I allow Him to do His work in me, He restores what I have absentmindedly damaged.

Week Thirty, Day 4

Continuing to learn from the life of Michal (wife of King David), I would like to examine 2 Samuel 6:20, which reads: "When David returned home to bless his household, Michal daughter of Saul came out to meet him and said, 'How the king of Israel has distinguished himself today, going around half-naked in full view of the slave girls of his servants as any vulgar fellow would!'"

David had returned home to bless his family. Was Michal about to be blessed? It seems as if she was, since she was a member of David's family. Yet she did not know David's intentions and she did not wait to find them out.

Instead, she bolted out the door to meet him – or perhaps to berate him? She let him know exactly what she thought of his actions, holding back none of her disgust.

How often do we forsake our blessings because we bolt ahead to gripe and complain? How often do we assume to know so much about a situation, only to discover that we really knew nothing at all?

What a terrible trade we so often make. We trade our blessings for bitterness, fellowship for loneliness, the joy of the Lord for misery. All because we rush ahead with our assumptions.

Slow down, listen to the Lord and to others, and be a woman who forsakes a bitter heart. Be blessed instead.

Week Thirty, Day 5

Do you ever have a verse or passage from the Bible jump out at you, and you are certain that the Lord wants you to memorize it?

If so, then great! You are in the Word and the Holy Spirit is speaking to you through Scripture!

If not, do not despair. Open your Bible, pray and ask the Lord to touch you from His Word, and expect to hear from Him. Old Testament or New Testament, take your pick. He will meet you there in the pages of your Bible

What if you have heard His call to memorize some portion of the Bible, hiding it safely in your heart, but you have not done the work of actually committing it to memory? Start today – do not delay any longer!

Memorizing verses that the Lord has laid upon our hearts is one of the most important, lasting and beneficial things we can ever do.

The blessings are for us, for our husbands and our children, our future grandchildren, our churches…and on it goes from there! Don't trade such a huge treasure trove of blessing due to laziness.

This one thing could have a massive impact on every single area of your life. Memorize God's Word!

Week Thirty-one, Day 1

The early years of child rearing are so jam-packed that they feel as if they will never end. Diapering alone seems never ending! So do midnight feedings and potty training. But as busy as those years are, and as slowly as the days crawl by, they really will come to an end. And it will come quickly, suddenly, like a thief in the night.

Dear mothers, hear me when I say this: these are precious moments in time and when they are gone, you will wish you had them back again.

I remember fussy babies, sicknesses that just kept recycling through our family, feeling as if I had not showered or been outside my front door in weeks. But I also chose to live according to Isaiah 40:11, which says He gently leads those that have young ones. If I was not being gently led during those years, then I simply didn't do it or I stopped doing it ASAP. It was that simple, and it really did work.

There was enough for me to do day by day. I did not need anything more piled upon my plate. Looking back, I am so glad that Isaiah 40:11 was my life motto. It was worth heeding day by day.

All that is said to remind you that the old adage "The days are long but the years are short" is true. So very true.

Use Isaiah 40:11 as your guide and those short years will be ones you reflect upon with thankfulness.

Week Thirty-one, Day 2

2 Timothy 4:2c – correct, rebuke and encourage – with great patience and careful instruction.

I truly love this verse from 2 Timothy. It is a beautiful reminder that God is involved in my life as a mother, wife, homeschooler. He wants me to provide my children with good teaching. That goes far beyond my curriculum choices and deals with my heart. Is my attitude right? Am I thankful for the time I have with my children today? Am I teaching from a Biblical worldview? Or have I allowed humanism to creep into our homeschool lessons? Am I willing to follow the Holy Spirit's leading, or do I feel the need to bend the knee to my to-do list and my lesson plans? Lesson planning and organization are good things, but they must take their place behind God's leadership and authority in our homes.

Am I patiently correcting and rebuking my children? Or am I nagging and pushing and shoving them along? Do I seek the Lord's will for them, or a will of my own choosing? Worse yet, do I leave room for the world's will for their lives?

I cannot make everyone happy, and God does not want me to keep on trying. Wouldn't I rather be a woman who pleases the Lord?

Trust Him today as you patiently correct, rebuke, encourage and teach your children.

Galatians 6:7- Do not be deceived: God cannot be mocked. A man reaps what he sows.

Read the above verse over a few of times.

Now, think of each of the children you are homeschooling.

Did you know that you will reap in each child's life exactly what you sow in them as their mother?

Do a quick Fill-in-the-Blank. I will reap in _____ 's life exactly what I sow. Ponder this regarding each or your children.

Understand that this is a Biblical truth. It is immutable and unchangeable. It will work as God has said it will work.

Choose daily to sow what you want to harvest. Be loving. Extend mercy. Model kindness. Teach patience. Don't smother. Try not to nag. Pray for your children. Teach them God's Word.

Enjoy the harvest one day by planting good seed today!

Isaiah 66:13a – As a mother comforts her children, so will I comfort you.

God is a comforter. Of all the descriptions He gives us of Himself, perhaps the knowledge that He promises to comfort is the one I relate to best. Being a mother is a unique privilege. All aspects of motherhood are unique, in fact. Our role as our children's primary comforter is just one example of our uniqueness.

And to think that our comforting nature is actually a reflection of our loving God! What an amazing, overwhelming truth to grasp.

How does a mother comfort her children? With physical attentiveness, coupled with verbal love and care, and a sure sense that even were the whole world to turn against you, even then you would still have your mother's love. And that is, in very limited fashion, the way our God loves each one of us.

Be a mother who loves well. And be God's child, well-loved by Him.

Week Thirty-one, Day 5

Job 5:21 – You will be protected from the lash of the tongue, and need not fear when destruction comes.

Homeschooling can be an open door for people's comments and criticism. There is no way to prevent it or hide from it; it's inevitable. The only real option is to find a way to deal with it.

Job 5:21 gives us a real life, solid verse to pray in order to strengthen us in advance of questions and criticism. We can ask Him to protect us from the lash of the tongue.

If you have a situation coming up wherein you know you will be hearing all about the negative aspects of homeschooling, then pray this verse in advance. It will strengthen you and often will quiet the words of the offenders.

If it is a sudden situation, pray this verse on the fly. God hears those prayers and answers them too – and you will hold your tongue as you are praying, which lessens the odds of you giving an un-Christ like reply.

Accept the reality that as homeschoolers, you will be questioned, and then accept the far greater reality that God will protect you from the lash of the tongue.

Week Thirty-two, Day 1

Romans 13:12a – The night is nearly over; the day is almost here.

In the darkest moments of our lives, when it seems the weight of our troubles will never be lifted, we can remember the promise found in Romans 13:12. The night is nearly over.

Every night comes to its end, and day breaks anew. So it is with our troubles. They end. It's a promise from the Lord God Almighty, and He keeps every single promise He has ever made.

Whether the day breaks in this life or when we step into eternity, it will happen. The heartache and pain and agony will cease. Your living God will see you through.

Stick close to Him. Remember His promise and watch for the dawn. And if you happen to be walking the full light of day right now, pray for someone who is not. We travel the road of life best when we walk with others who love the Lord.

The day is almost here.

Week Thirty-two, Day 2

Worry is a prison that contaminates the "right now" and also damages the future. It distorts and taints the past. No part of your life is exempt or safe from the side-effects of your fretting. We all know how much damage is done by worrying – and yet we all keep doing it.

What would your life look like if you did not worry? Okay – I can almost hear you groaning that I cannot seriously expect you to never worry again. But I can ask you to set aside worrying just for today. That's not unreasonable, is it?

One day at a time, we can choose not to worry. And what a different life we live when we do!

I remember when the Lord laid it upon my heart to give up worrying for forty straight days. I thought it was impossible! But as it turns out, those forty days were some of the best of my life. I would write "No Worrying" at the top of my to-do list every day, and if I caught myself fretting, I set aside the worry out of obedience to the Lord. It truly changed my life.

So today, do not worry. Your Father has it all under control.

Week Thirty-two, Day 3

Ecclesiastes 5:19b-20 – To enjoy your work and to accept your lot in life – that is indeed a gift from God. People who do this rarely look with sorrow on the past, for God has given them reasons for joy. (New Living Translation)

This verse provides an answer to the nagging question, "Why do I feel so unsatisfied with life?" We have all asked it at some point or another. Sleepless nights, days when household chores seem to never end, times when every school lesson takes forever and no progress is made.

On days like this, I find the cure is to simply opt to enjoy my lot in life, no matter what that lot may be at the moment. And that one switch from a complaining spirit to a thankful one changes everything. It really is a gift from God, just as this verse says. But it's not a gift I can enjoy if I never bother to open it.

But once I do open the gift, I find myself no longer looking back to Lake Woebegone Days or straining forward toward a more peaceful future. I am able to see the reasons for joy that God has blessed me with right here and now, and all my sorrows and lamenting seem silly.

Why not try it for yourself? Enjoy your work and accept your lot in life with a thankful heart, for God has given you reasons for joy!

Week Thirty-two, Day 4

I once read this quote: "God can do great things through someone whose mind is like fertile soil."

It has reminded me of what I hope for in my children as I homeschool them. Not a closed mind, not a doubtful mind, not a stubborn mind; these are all like dry, hard, rocky soil. But fertile soil, that is what I want their minds to be like.

It is also how the Lord wants my mind to be. Soft and pliable and ready to receive from Him. Combine this with a tender heart that loves Him and that makes for a teachable woman.

It's easy to become dry and hard, unwilling to learn from the Lord. But He is gracious and longs for us to stay open to Him on a continual basis.

Ask Him to keep you tender toward Him and His will, and then prepare to see what great things he can do through you.

Week Thirty-two, Day 5

Psalm 90:17 – May the favor of the Lord our God rest upon us; establish the work of our hands for us.

Ask God what you ought to do and then do not hesitate to do it. As you do this, the work of your hands (namely homeschooling) will be better established.

I can think of very little I would rather experience than the favor and the blessing of the Lord. With His favor, I can face the toughest day of homeschooling, the most intimidating academic subjects, the very worst of sick days, and an empty dinner table at 6pm!

Psalm 90:17 makes an excellent prayer for the busy homeschooling mother. Cry out to the Lord, asking Him to establish the work of your hands today. Seek His favor upon your life, your family, your home. Be watching for His answer. He will bless the work of your hands.

Week Thirty-three, Day 1

<u>Proverbs 12:25</u> – Anxiety weighs down the heart, but a kind word cheers it up.

Our lives as homeschooling mothers can be filled with concerns. Have you considered that our children can also be full of worry?

They may have worries all their own, or they may take on the worries of their parents. Sadly, we may not even notice. If we would but take the time, we could easily see their worried hearts.

When worry overtakes our children, there is hope and comfort we can offer from God's Word. The solution to their worry will always be the encouragement and safety found in the Bible.

In addition, our encouragement and love can help them navigate their scary moments. Of course they need to learn to rely on the Lord's great love as they grow and mature in Christ. But they also need someone with "skin on", so to speak, who can love and encourage them as well. Be that someone when your children are afraid.

Thank them for their help with household chores, tell them when they have done well academically, give them a hug and tell them you love them. They will be encouraged, and so will you.

Week Thirty-three, Day 2

Numbers 9:23 – At the Lord's command they encamped, and at the Lord's command they set out. They obeyed the Lord's order, in accordance with his command through Moses.

One of my favorite times of the year is our annual family vacation. We have ventured to many destinations over the years, and we have a tradition of purchasing a magnet at each unique place. All those magnets stuck to our fridge serve as an ample reminder of all those family trips! But there have been years when we have not been able to take a trip as a family. And those years remind me of Numbers 9, verse 23.

Being at home instead of on a summer trip isn't necessarily a bad thing. Like Moses, who truly developed an obedient heart, we have had times when we stayed put because that was what the Lord willed for us.

Whether or not you are afforded the opportunity to travel together as a family, you can still be blessed when you obey the Lord as Moses did. Always be willing to stay or to go at God's command, and know that His greatest blessings come for those who are quick to obey.

Obedience brings blessing, never forget that. Move at the Lord's command, and rest at the Lord's command. Be blessed as you live your life at the pace He gives you.

Week Thirty-one, Day 3

Psalms 125:2 – As the mountains surround Jerusalem, so the Lord surrounds his people both now and forevermore.

You are surrounded. Completely and totally surrounded.

The Lord your God has surrounded you and your family today, and He will hold that position unwaveringly forevermore.

No matter what you are facing today, know with all certainty you do not face it alone. You have the One true God standing as your protective shield and covering.

Lift up your eyes and trust anew today in your King of kings and Lord of lords. Allow His perfect peace to keep you steadfast and secure. Rejoice in Him who longs to do the impossible, showing Himself strong on your behalf.

Be blessed today, fellow homeschooling mother, and remember – He has you surrounded.

2 Corinthians 9:8 – God is able to make all grace abound to you, so that in all times, having all that you need, you will abound in every good work.

From living on a single income to coping with lay-offs; purchasing curriculum and paying for car repairs. Planning affordable but healthy meals and funding family travels. Homeschoolers learn to depend on God's abounding grace for all that they need.

When we homeschool, it affords us many opportunities for God to prove Himself faithful. Have you stopped and asked Him to make your life and your family and even your homeschool into a platform that showcases His faithfulness?

When we are careful to leave plenty of room for God to act in our every circumstance, we find that not only does He give us all that we need. We also see firsthand that He means for us to abound in every good work.

If we're not abounding, it certainly is not because His promise is untrue. Reevaluate why you may be struggling; bring your doubts into the light. And open your heart fully to His abundance.

Week Thirty-three, Day 5

Are you keeping your husband in his rightful place?

It is very easy to become ensnared by all-things-homeschool. That is why we must fight against it. The current will take you wherever it wills so long as you are willing to simply drift along.

Homeschooling is a great thing! Our children are precious gifts from the Lord. But where do our husbands fit in?

Here is a little litmus test to gauge your husband's place in your home.

How many magazine and newsletters about homeschooling do you subscribe to? And how much attention do you pay to your husband's favorite hobby, or even to his career?

Do you ever find yourself staying up late reading homeschool blogs or looking at things on Pinterest? While you are up late, where is your husband? If he is going to bed alone, something is out of place.

What's most important to your husband? What are you doing to make his priorities your priorities? If you do not know what his priorities are, you may need to start there.

Don't let homeschooling rob your husband of his rightful place in your life!

Week Thirty-four, Day 1

<u>1 Peter 5:7</u> – Cast all your anxiety on him because he cares for you.

I truly love this verse. On any given day, in any possible situation, it is applicable. It's like a well-worn soft hoodie; it always fits just right.

All my anxiety – all your anxiety – all the anxiety of our children. ALL. What a word those three letters create! And what a Savior, who ensures we know this promise is within the reach of every one of us. Anything that creates an anxious heart in us can be cast upon the Lord. It is perfectly okay and even expected that we roll it all right onto Him.

Here's the catch: the promise only applies to us if we actually cast our anxiety on Him. If we sort of set it down close to Him, attach it to ourselves with a bungee cord and walk away dragging it with us…well, then we fail to do what the verse instructs us to do.

So cast it all on Him and let His love and His care flood over you today.

Colossians 3:2a – Let heaven fill your thoughts. (New Living Translation)

If you are discouraged or even depressed, perhaps you have not been letting heaven fill your thoughts. It may be time for a thought-life sabbatical.

Take authority over what you think about. Start by considering what voices you are hearing predominantly. Too much talk radio that isn't Biblical and encouraging? Don't listen. The nightly news bringing you down? Turn off the television. A neighbor that catches you watering your lawn and gripes in your ear every evening? Set up the sprinkler and tell her you have some things to do in the house.

Is your reading material God-honoring? If not, close the book and find a different one. The lady at the homeschool co-op is depressed and her gloominess is wearing you out? Write her a note with some encouraging verses and tell her you will be praying for her, and then pour out nothing but positive in greater measure than her negative. If that fails, distance yourself form her. You can even tell her why, if you need to.

Then be sure to think about heaven to replace the old negative stuff you're no longer thinking about. We will be there forever, after all, so we probably should be looking forward to it with excitement.

Week Thirty-four, Day 3

<u>Romans 12:11</u> – Never be lazy in your work, but serve the Lord enthusiastically. (New Living Translation)

Dear homeschooling mother –how I wish I could share the lessons I have learned regarding personal laziness…but sadly, I probably have not fully learned those lessons and am not really equipped to share with you.

What I want to learn more fully is how to make my time the Lord's time in every area of my life. For me, therein lies the antidote to laziness.

I have, at times, been able to muster up the strength to serve the Lord enthusiastically for brief moments. But then my flesh sets in my enthusiasm wanes, and I fail at this endeavor. All because I attempt to live the Christian life in my own strength and ability.

Today, leaning fully on Him, trusting He will provide all the energy and wisdom and joy that I need, I hope to do His will with more enthusiasm. Today, I ask Him to remove any lazy tendencies and awaken my heart to His strength. And today, I am certain he will answer these prayers and move me closer to a resemblance of Him.

Week Thirty-four, Day 4

Matthew 28:20b – And surely I am with you always, to the very end of the age.

This is both a verse of comfort and promise. And it also serves as a reminder that this earth is not our home.

When the end of the age finally comes, we want what we've invested our limited resource of time in to be the right investments. The very best possible investments.

As homeschoolers we can forget that the *real* big picture is Jesus…not homeschooling. We are eternal beings, the same as every other person on this planet. One day we will all step into eternity. It is far more important to take as many people with us to our new home with Jesus than it is to squabble over things that do not matter in light of eternity.

Don't become so focused on your homeschool world that you neglect the rest of the lost world around you. Keep eternity in your heart and mind and care about people above all else.

<u>Romans 12:15-16a</u> – Rejoice with those who rejoice; mourn with those who mourn. Live in harmony with one another.

Homeschoolers don't always have the day-by-day interaction with people that others may experience. Many days we never even leave the house. So how can we live out Romans 12:15-16?

Start within your own home. If your child is happy about, say, their art project, then be happy along with them. Listen with your head and your heart as they show you over and over again all the ins and outs of their favorite toy. And genuinely smile with happiness for them! They know when you don't really mean it.

If one of your children is sad, perhaps about their difficulty understanding a new math concept, then feel their sadness and just be sad right alongside them. This is harmonious homeschool living.

And then, when you're at the library, church, or even the grocery store, apply this verse more broadly. Smile at the checkout girl who is clearly discouraged. Let the gentleman with an armful of packages step in front of you in line at the post office. Congratulate your husband's buddy on his big promotion.

Engaging in people's lives truly shows that you care, reminds them that God cares, and promotes peaceful living.

Week Thirty-five, Day 1

Galatians 6:9 – Let us not become weary in doing good, for at the proper time we will reap a harvest if we do not give up.

The harvest. It can seem so far off during the early years of homeschooling. Yet when you reach the end point and pause to look back, it will seem as if the time flew by in the blink of an eye. It was here a moment ago…and now it's gone. Just like that.

How can it seem so different in the end than it did in the beginning?

Everyone faces this bitter reality. Time is a slow drudgery and also a speedy haste. Remembering that both truths will one day collide helps prepare us for the changes ahead and keeps us focused on the here and now.

If we can learn how to not grow weary as we seek to do good, we will be able to catch glimpses of the rewards that we will reap. Don't lose heart if you are in the midst of the early, long years of homeschooling. The harvest comes later, and it is worth the wait.

Are you a long-term homeschooling mother? If so, have you noticed that there is quite a bit of reading material aimed at encouraging new homeschoolers and not so much for those who have been at it for quite some time?

Long-term homeschoolers need to be encouraged, too. I say this as a mother who writes with the sole purpose of encouraging women who homeschool their children. You could say it is my "job" to encourage others. But believe it or not, even though this is my main purpose in writing, I still need to be encouraged myself.

In fact, as I look to the near future when my nest will be empty, I find I need to be encouraged more and more frequently.

Often I look to the writing of the heroes of the faith who have gone before me. The works of C.H. Spurgeon, A.W. Tozer, Watchman Nee, E.M. Bounds and A.B. Simpson push and pull and move me along, giving me the encouragement I so often need.

There are also modern-day heroes of the faith whose writing I frequently read, such as Anne Graham Lotz and Joni Ericson Tada and Jennifer Kennedy Dean and Susie Larson. These authors pen words that are key in my daily desire to mature in Christ.

Be sure to keep looking for sources of encouragement, whether you are a new homeschooler or one who is about to have an empty nest. And then, be a source of encouragement for someone else today.

Be careful not to allow yourself to become judgmental of others – either in your thoughts or in your words!

It is so easy to feel like a superior and more dedicated mother when you homeschool. To think, "I do more for my children than so-and-so, she just hands them lunch money and shoves them out the door and onto the big yellow school bus."

At its core, this attitude is judgmental. And it is sin.

I am not the judge of my neighbor or the women at church or my sister-in-law or anyone else. They have one judge, the Righteous Judge, and He is a perfect judge of all things. To take His place as judge in my attitude toward others is a grievous sin. I must take that sin seriously.

Choose the words that you speak about others with great care, as you will one day give an account for every idle word you speak. And guard your thoughts. If you find yourself thinking in a judgmental manner about someone, then pause and pray (right at that very moment) and ask the Lord to take those thoughts and make them obedient to Him.

Be shrewd about your own ability to cast judgment. And be open to let God govern your words and your thoughts.

2 Samuel 16:22 – So they pitched a tent for Absalom on the roof, and he slept with his father's concubines in the sight of all Israel.

David was a man after God's own heart. He was Israel's most famous king and also the youngest of his brothers, the one who slew the giant Goliath with a sling and a stone. Yet despite having the Lord's favor resting upon him, King David had many wives and concubines. David surely knew this was not God's best for him, but for some reason he decided to do things his own way rather than God's ideal way.

It also appears that David may have had some trouble disciplining his children (see 2 Samuel 13, 15 and 16 for examples of this). Any reason I present for David's seeming neglect in this aspect of his parenting would be pure speculation, but I cannot help but wonder if the problem predated his children. Perhaps the problem began with the many mothers of his many children?

If we fail to discipline our children, they will suffer. And if we fail to deal with our own parasitic sins, our children may be forced to deal with those same sins in their own lives. What evidence do I have to support this notion? 2 Samuel 16:21-23. What David had done in secret, his son Absalom did in the full light of day for all to see.

When our children grow up watching particular sins being repeated over and over again, it becomes very easy for them to take those sins to an even more brazen level and think nothing of it. Praise God, this is not always the case! Our God is always able and willing to deliver children from generational sin. But I do not want to test Him in this, nor do I want my children to fight any more spiritual battles than is needed to make them like Christ.

May we desire to leave a heritage of godliness to our children, and may we settle for nothing less.

Week Thirty-five, Day 5

Numbers 6:24-27 – The Lord bless you and keep you, the Lord make his face shine on you and be gracious to you; the Lord turn his face toward you and give you peace. So they will put my name on the Israelites, and I will bless them.

At the start of each new homeschool year, I spend time seeking the Lord and asking Him to give me some specific verses for our family. And each year He does just that. It is remarkable to watch Him do marvelous things in our homeschool and in our family, things that so often correspond perfectly with the Bible verses He laid upon my heart before the year began.

This academic year was different. Although I had been praying about verses for our homeschool year all summer long, I had not received anything from the Lord. Here it was, the first day of school...and still I had nothing. As I read my Bible that morning, I came upon Numbers 6:24-27. Such beautiful verses of hope and promise. God had provided His Word for our school year.

God is never late, and He never will be. You can trust Him to provide in every way at all times, even for something like annual Bible verses for your homeschool. He is not neglectful, and He is never in a rush. Keep trusting Him for all that you need, and don't be surprised if at times He reveals Himself at the very last moment.

"He (God) is not wanting great men, but He is wanting men who will dare to prove the greatness of their God." – A.B. Simpson

When I pray over my husband each day, I ask the Lord for very specific things. The exact requests may vary from day to day, but I always aim to be specific. Vague prayers are far more difficult to discern the answers to, and if we are uncertain God answered our prayers then we are not very likely to thank Him for answering. Specific prayers, which often have specific answers, are far more noticeable. This lends itself to profuse thankfulness. Part of why I pray very specifically is to spur on a more grateful attitude in my own heart.

Some days I will pray and ask the Lord to use my husband, or my children, or even myself to prove His greatness. Over the course of our day, in any manner He sees fit, to take our weakness and exalt Himself through us. Proving His greatness by doing His will through my little family. This is a wonderful prayer that I have found God delights in answering.

What about you, homeschooling mother? Would you be willing to let the Lord prove His greatness through your family, your homeschool, your life? Can you pray that He will do this in your husband's life?

Be brave enough to fully live the life that God has given you, and ask Him to prove just how great a God He is through you today.

Week Thirty-six, Day 2

<u>Job 27:1</u> – I will teach you about the power of God; the ways of the Almighty I will not conceal.

One of the best parts of homeschooling for a Christian mother is the ability to teach our children about the Lord every day of their growing-up years. We always have opportunity to share from God's Word and to talk about the awesome things God has done in our own lives. There is no end to the Christian biographies we can read aloud from, telling our children of wonders too astounding to land on the pages of a fiction novel...and yet they are all true.

When we take Job's words to heart and choose to teach our children about the power of God, we have chosen the better part and it will surely not be lost on our youngsters. As we grow in our understanding of the Lord and His ways, we should share what we learn with our family. Growing together as we walk with Him is one major thing that homeschoolers can do better than most anyone else. We truly can talk about Him all day long, when we rise and when we sit and as we go about our daily duties.

Decide that you will not conceal the ways of the Almighty. Become a family who is continually growing in the Lord.

Psalm 25:12, 14 – Who, then, are those who fear the Lord? He will instruct them in the ways they should choose. ~ The Lord confides in those who fear him; he makes his covenant known to them.

A healthy fear of the Lord will always acknowledge His goodness as well as His greatness. He is indeed a very good God, full of compassion, slow to anger and abounding in love.

He is also a very great God, holy and righteous and completely without sin. He will discipline when it is needed, and He will not tolerate open rebellion or hardness of heart. Our God is always perfect in His justice, as He is perfect in His love.

When we understand more about Who God is, we are developing a healthy fear of the Lord. And in Psalm 25 we are promised that when we fear Him, He will instruct us in all the ways we should choose. The plural word "ways" is used here, indicating that we can depend on His instruction over and over and over again throughout our lives. What a blessing to know this truth!

Fear the Lord, and hear from Him. He will confide in you, and He will make His promises known to you.

Ecclesiastes 10:11 – It does no good to charm a snake after it has bitten you. (New Living Translation)

Have you ever felt the sting of some offense which you did not see coming? Something painful that you did not expect? Have you ever been terribly hurt when something went awry after you had invested so much? All wounds hurt, but this kind of pain is unique. It seems to hurt worse when we have poured so much of ourselves into something, doesn't it?

In regard to our journey as homeschoolers, this verse reminds me to be cautious and aware; to guard my heart! We are called to love everyone, and we must do what Jesus taught. But He does not ask us to give all of ourselves to everyone in our lives. We must give what He asks us to give, but we should not give more than He asks us to give. At times we will be stretched to give more than we are comfortable with, but we obey our Lord and give anyway. Other times we sense Him leading us to hold back a little bit, and this is often His means of protecting us from harm. We must always listen to the Holy Spirit and do things His way.

Be careful not to pour all of your heart into every single relationship. After all, some people may not be able to handle all of your passion and the results could be painful for everyone involved.

Don't withdraw from and neglect relationships. But do remember Jesus' words in Matthew 7:6 "Do not give dogs what is sacred; do not throw your pearls to pigs. If you do, they may trample them under their feet, and turn and tear you to pieces." Don't pass judgment on others or become hard-hearted and hateful. Just don't give all of yourself to everyone in your life. If we lived our lives giving 100% of all we are to everyone around us, we would be exhausted and so would they!

By searching God's Word and looking at verses like Ecclesiastes 10:11 and Matthew 7:6 side by side, we are better able to live our lives God's way. Dig into the Word today and discover what He wants you to learn.

Psalm 16:6 – The boundary lines have fallen for me in pleasant places; surely I have a delightful inheritance.

Of all the things the Lord has taught me during my two decades of homeschooling, hands-down the most valuable thing has been that He truly wants me to enjoy my life.

My husband and my children and the ability to homeschool are all gifts that He has given to me. Why would He give me a gift and then not want me to enjoy it? That would not make any sense at all.

Yet, in my own natural state, I find that it is very difficult for me to enjoy my life. I have struggled with this quite a bit, and I suspect I am not the only mother who feels this way. A twinge of guilt about being genuinely happy, a sense of dread that I am somehow not a holy enough woman if I am not pious and serious much of the time.

But are these ideas true? Do they align with what God says in the Bible? If the joy of the Lord is my strength, am I trading my strength for weakness when I refuse to enjoy my life?

Psalm 16:6 has become one of my absolute favorite verses from the Bible. It reminds me that He has given me ample reasons for great joy. He has made my boundary lines fall in pleasant places. This life is good. It is His good gift to me. And I am allowed to enjoy it.

And so are you.

Notes:

Notes:

Made in the USA
San Bernardino, CA
20 November 2015